SUMMER SPORTS CAMPS 101

Titles in the Sport Management Library

For an updated list of Sport Management Library titles, please visit

www.fitpublishing.com

SUMMER SPORTS CAMPS 101
A Guidebook for Development and Operation

Richard Leonard, PhD

PUBLISHING

FiT Publishing
A DIVISION OF THE INTERNATIONAL CENTER FOR PERFORMANCE EXCELLENCE
375 Birch Street, WVU-CPASS • PO Box 6116
Morgantown, WV 26506-6116
www.fitpublishing.com

Library of Congress Card Catalog Number: 2015933054

ISBN: 978-1-940067-03-2

Cover Design: 40 West Studios

Cover Photos: Main photo: Photographerlondon I Dreamstime.com I Coach in Front of Girl Soccer Players Photo, Supplementary Photos: WVU Photo Services

Production Editor: Nita Shippy

Copyeditor: Geoffrey Fuller

Proofreader: Matt Brann

Indexer: Matt Brann

Typesetter: 40 West Studios

Printed by: Publishers' Graphics

10 9 8 7 6 5 4 3 2 1

FiT Publishing
A Division of the International Center for Performance Excellence
West Virginia University
375 Birch Street, WVU-CPASS
PO Box 6116
Morgantown, WV 26506-6116
800.477.4348 (toll free)
304.293.6888 (phone)
304.293.6658 (fax)
Email: fitcustomerservice@mail.wvu.edu
Website: www.fitpublishing.com

Contents

Detailed Table of Contents

SECTION II: PLANNING   29

SECTION III: ADMINISTRATION SYSTEMS   55

SECTION V: MARKETING SYSTEMS   113

SECTION VI: RISK MANAGEMENT AND SPORT CAMP OPERATIONS   149

Foreword

I am introducing this book from the perspective of a person who is both an educator and who has owned and operated a specialized sports training camp in the north woods of Wisconsin. Olympia Sports Village was the site of training camps conducted initially on a year-round basis and later during the summer months. As such, I had more than a passing interest in the book authored by Dr. Richard Leonard titled, *Summer Sports Camps 101: A Guidebook for Development and Operation.*

With my experience as a backdrop, I found his treatment of the subject to be comprehensive. More importantly, I appreciated the practical examples that served to illuminate the explanation of various operating situations that one typically encounters in putting together these kinds of short-term, yet intensive, training programs. The numerous tips in the margins of the text also serve to enrich the chapters of the book and the appendixes offer specific facts and supporting documents, such as the laws applicable to summer camp operations. The 200+ pages in the text are logically divided into major sections including planning, administrative systems, human resources, marketing and very importantly, risk management.

On the whole, the book is well written, very readable, and should serve as an indispensable guide for those individuals considering organizing summer camps for the first time and holds helpful tips for those who have already done so.

Thomas P. Rosandich, PhD
President and CEO
United States Sports Academy

INTRODUCTION

Running a summer sports camp can be personally gratifying and financially profitable. Camps can provide athletic organizations with new resources and capabilities, increased public awareness, and the foundations for new program recruits. However, they must not be entered into lightly. They take time, perseverance, and mental and physical exertion to operate correctly.

To decide whether or not to develop and manage a summer sports camp, one should complete a feasibility study that examines the practicality of the venture. If this initial step looks promising, tools such as an external environmental investigation, a competitive analysis, and a SWOT breakdown should be employed to determine the potential camp's possibilities.

1

Launching a Summer Sports Camp

WHY RUN A SUMMER SPORTS CAMP?

The reasons are as varied as the people involved, but generally are grouped into two types: *internal* and *external* rewards. Internal rewards, also known as *intrinsic rewards,* are defined as "rewards internal to the individual and normally derived from involvement in certain activities and tasks."[1] In other words, internal rewards are the good feelings brought on by participating in actions that one feels are beneficial to oneself or others. Conversely, external rewards, also known as *extrinsic rewards,* are defined as behaviors that are "performed to acquire material or social rewards or to avoid punishment; the source of motivation is the consequences of the behavior, not the behavior itself."[2] The clear outcome of externally motivated behavior is financial, often in the form of a paycheck or benefits.

In reality, individuals are usually motivated by a combination of internal and external rewards. In fact, the combination is essential for one to be both internally motivated and financially satisfied—two key ingredients in any successful business undertaking.

If a summer sports camp is a part of an athletic department in an academic institution (to be discussed later in the chapter), the measurable benefits and intangible advantages can be substantial.

Additional Resources for the Athletic Program

Anyone who has spent time in athletic program administration or coaching understands how critical budgets and fiscal accountability are. Unfortunately, a majority of athletic program budgets lack funding in significant categories—sometimes the shortfalls are severe. The operation of a profitable summer sports camp often can lessen, if not completely eliminate, certain shortages. With a stronger financial core, an athletic program can experience a stronger competitive advantage, which, in turn, can contribute to wins and program stability.

Supplement Coaches' Salaries

A significant key to any athletic program's success is the quality of its coaching staff. As with all free market personnel decisions, having a "blue chip" employee requires strong monetary incentives. A thriving camp operation can provide these sources of revenue to convince quality coaches to join and stay in the program.

Evaluating Talent

Recruiting is considered the lifeblood of an athletic organization. A considerable "off the balance sheet" benefit of a summer sports camp is the ability to evaluate potential program athletes in a controlled camp environment. Having prospects and recruits involved in an extensive athletic program sports camp provides far more detail into an athlete's abilities than other possible recruiting methods. Coaches and program staff can observe first-hand an athlete's athleticism, attitude, work ethic, teamwork, and overall suitability for athletic program inclusion.

Program Goodwill and Community Engagement

Goodwill is primarily a product of a business's value and reputation. A well run sports camp can have a tremendous impact on an athletic program's goodwill and community involvement. By running a sports camp, the increase in an athletic program's appeal to the community will be a natural byproduct. Often, a camp will provide the athletic program with a group of trusted community members who are dedicated supporters for years beyond their camp involvement.

Increased Brand Awareness

Branding is critical for developing a stable and growing customer base. How potential customers (in the case of sports, fans and supporters) feel about an athletic organization can be directly connected with their brand familiarity. Willia Perreault, Joseph Cannon, and Jerome McCarthy, in their 2012 book, *Essentials of Marketing*, describe five levels of brand familiarity:

Camp Tip

The athletic program's governing body will have detailed contact and evaluation rules when it comes to potential recruits. Whether an athletic program is in the NCAA, NAIA, NJCAA, or a state high school athletic association, a sports camp administrator must know all relevant policies and procedures relating to recruiting and summer camp operations.

- **Brand rejection** means that potential customers won't buy a brand unless its image is changed. . . . [O]vercoming a negative image is difficult and can be very expensive.

- **Brand nonrecognition** means final consumers don't recognize the brand at all.

- **Brand recognition** means that the customer remembers the brand. This may not seem like much, but it can be a big advantage if there are many "nothing" brands on the market.

- **Brand preference** means that target customers usually choose the brand over other brands, perhaps because of habit or favorable past experiences.

- **Brand insistence** means customers insist on a firm's branded product and are willing to search for it.[3]

The ultimate goal of any operation is to achieve the brand familiarity level of brand insistence. Athletic organizations are no different. Well-developed summer sports camps can help an athletic program increase the public's familiarity with the program, making it *the* program the public thinks of first—branding the program in the public's eyes. There are many ways this can happen. First, promotional tactics for the summer sports camp can be tied directly to the athletic program's overall promotional campaign. Second, a camp, if beneficial and enjoyable, will not only influence the participant toward brand insistence, but it can also influence the participants' family and friends. Finally, a camp participant can (and should) be a part of the athletic program's contact database. Through the use of newsletters, web links, emails, and social media, the participant can become more invested in the athletic program. The more invested one is, the higher the level of brand insistence and support.

Learning Community of Coaches

An often unnoticed benefit of running a camp relates to coaching development and training. A well-run and high-quality camp can bring in coaching talent from all over the country, and even the world. This pool of gifted coaches can foster an atmosphere of sports learning for all people involved with the camp. Whether through casual conversations, open discussion, free-associating sessions, or formal developmental activities, techniques that are cultivated during a summer sports camp can become an important part of a coach's in-season training method and competitive plans.

Other Related Benefits

Other advantages of operating a strong camp for an athletic program can encompass the following:

- possible media coverage and positive public relations through human interest stories;

- educating the community on a sport, if it is not considered mainstream;

Camp Tip

If an athletic organization, through its sports camp, can get participants to the brand familiarity level of insistence, they often become vocal supporters of the athletic program. This, in turn, will generate positive word-of-mouth promotions that can increase attendance, support, and recruiting.

- promotion of the overall educational institution where the camp is being held; and
- building and strengthening ties with current and potential strategic alliances.

An entrepreneur is defined as "one who creates a new business in the face of risk and uncertainty for the purpose of achieving profit and growth by identifying significant opportunities and assembling the necessary resources to capitalize on them."[4] If a camp is an entrepreneurial venture, the benefits to an individual or group can also be considerable. Some of the distinct personal and professional gains that can be experienced by a sports camp entrepreneur include the following:

Personal Satisfaction and Independence

By operating an independent camp, an individual can experience deep personal satisfaction by having power over his or her professional future. In most cases, major incentives for individuals operating entrepreneurial ventures are the autonomy and the feeling of control over one's professional destiny. This is no different for individuals or groups who conduct sports camps.

New Professional Opportunities

A basic fact of business is that all careers plateau. If one is in a profession outside of athletics and is dissatisfied with one's career path, a potential way to break into a sports career as a coach or athletic program administrator is to get involved with or create and run an entrepreneurial sports camp. Besides all the intangible benefits, a camp is an excellent way to

- network inside a particular sport,
- find out about possible career opportunities,
- develop skills necessary for a career move, and, most importantly,
- discover if a career in athletics is the new direction one wants to go.

In general, sports camps, whether entrepreneurial or institutional, are great ways for an individual to participate and become immersed in a new career.

Financial Strategic Fit

While an entrepreneurial sports camp can be a stand-alone business with all of the profits going to the individual owners, it can also be an extension of a large-scale, year-round or in-season sports organization. For example, if the entrepreneurial business is a Junior Olympic or club program, a sports camp is a natural extension of that operation. Conversely, a strong and profitable camp operation can provide the financial resources to take on a new or develop an existing year-round or in-season program. In either instance, the participating athlete will have the advantage of continuity in training. The entrepreneurial venture will also have year-round financial balancing through additional revenue sources.

WHEN NOT TO RUN A SUMMER SPORTS CAMP

Chapter 2 will examine the mechanics and importance of feasibility studies. For now it is critical to understand that feasibility studies examine the tangible elements of a camp to help evaluate its viability. However, prior to analyzing the hard data, personal opinions and insights must be taken into account. It is beyond the scope of this book to determine every possible opinion-based motive for con-

sidering a camp, but some general factors might indicate that a sports camp should *not* be operated. These factors can be examined through firsthand observation, intuition, thoughtful evaluations, and years of sports-related experience.

Bottom-Line Only Thinking

The following is absolutely true when it comes to profit and entrepreneurship.

> The financial return of any business must compensate its owner for investing personal time (a salary equivalent) and personal savings (an interest and/or dividend equivalent) before true profits are realized. Entrepreneurs should expect a return that will not only compensate them for the time and money they invest but also reward them well for the risks and initiative they take in operating their own businesses. Indeed, some profit is necessary for a firm's survival.[5]

In spite of this fact, bottom-line only thinking is a central danger in running any business, summer sports camps included. If the one and only objective is profit, numerous internal and external issues will probably surface. Internally, monetary preoccupation in a business can

- influence dangerous cost cutting of vital operational elements,
- lead to micromanaging and reduced employee motivation,
- affect customer satisfaction through lower quality, and
- ultimately lead to a decline of the entire operation.

Externally, focusing on the bottom-line only can irreversibly damage an athletic organization's reputation and community goodwill. The cascading impact of this can have serious consequences on the athletic program for years to come.

It must be repeated that a camp needs to be profitable to survive. Nevertheless, a profit-first-and-foremost attitude is risky business. Instead, maintain a true desire to develop a quality camp that engages one's internal passion as well as fulfilling financial needs.

Time Commitment

Camps take a substantial amount of time to develop and operate, especially if they are new endeavors. If sufficient time cannot be committed to their formation, structure, staffing, and management, the camp will inevitably collapse and fail. Potential camp administrators need to take an unemotional look into their time availability and time-management skills. If they are unwilling or unable to commit sufficient time to the camp's operation, they should reconsider avoiding the idea of operating a camp.

Noticeable Operational Shortfalls

Business success is often determined by the effective use of organizational resources such as money, facilities and equipment, and human resources. To maximize resource use, an organization needs to access talent, skills, and capabilities, which requires a skills inventory. The basic principle behind a skills inventory is illustrated with the following formula:

Skills Required to Operate Business & Accomplish Goals –
Current Available Skills = Skills Needed

Obviously, in the best case, the current and future skills in the camp are the skills required to accomplish a camp's goals. In this case, the camp has no skill shortages. Conversely, in the worst-case scenario, none of the skills needed currently exist. The camp would be starting from scratch. The situation is even worse if there is no potential to acquire the needed skills in the future.

While all businesses have some degree of skill weaknesses and gaps, there are two major areas that are critical for sports camps: instructional and administrative skills. A camp's success and potential growth depends on the quality of instruction and the internal administrative talents of the operators. If, after a general inventory of skills required and skills available, one finds existing skills seriously lacking, one should reconsider or postpone the creation of the camp.

Observable Factors

When deciding whether or not to run a summer sports camp, there are some concrete factors that should be studied. The first is location. In their 2009 text *Small Business Management,* Byrd and Megginson identify five general location elements affecting all businesses:

1. Access to a capable, well-trained, and stable work force.

2. Availability of adequate and affordable supplies and services.

3. Availability, type, use, and cost of transportation.

4. Taxes and government regulations.

5. Availability and cost of electricity, gas, water, sewerage, and other utilities.[6]

Camp Tip

A general rule for sports camps: It is better not to run a camp than it is to run a poor one. The financial and public relations impact can be devastating to an athletic program or entrepreneur.

In addition to these general location points, camps also need to take into account the following:

- availability of safe and affordable athletic facilities and equipment;
- a central location that is accessible to all potential campers, faculty, and staff;
- proper housing and food services;
- parking and other camper drop-off areas; and
- image—appropriate and safe geographic locations.

While each situation is unique, all of these elements can severely damage a prospective camp.

Next, one must reflect on an overview of the competitive environment. While a feasibility study provides an in-depth competitive analysis, an uncomplicated review of the competitive environment is also helpful. If the general evaluation reveals a competitive environment that is oversupplied with well-run and long-established camps, then one needs to consider the potential camp's ability to

1. enter the market,
2. establish a position, and
3. develop core skills to establish a competitive advantage.

A final element to examine when considering a camp is the upfront financial resource commitment necessary to plan, structure, and staff a new venture. The financial requirements of a camp can be prohibitive. Costs such as marketing and promotions, facility deposits, staff and clinician guarantees, and miscellaneous administrative expenses are just a few of the possible upfront financial outlays. It is important to realize that most of these costs must be met well before any sources of revenue are obtained to offset them. This level of risk needs to be openly discussed with all interested parties; unquestionably, it is a conversation of risk versus potential rewards. The question becomes, if the worst case scenario happens, can the individuals, group, or organization absorb potential losses?

For the purpose of clarity, the next three sections (Recreational Camps Versus Instructional Camps, Entrepreneurial Ventures Versus Institutional Camps, and Day Camps Versus Night Camps) need to be explained.

RECREATIONAL CAMPS VERSUS INSTRUCTIONAL SPORTS CAMPS

It is important to note that camps are not all alike. The two types are *recreational* and *instructional* (in our case, sport instruction).

Recreational Camps

Some factors customarily associated with recreational camps include the following:

- Recreational camps are more entertainment based, with activities geared toward participant amusement and enjoyment.

- Recreational camps are characteristically associated with general child care.

- Recreational camps have larger target markets. The targeted customer groups have wider characteristics (demographic), encompass many different lifestyles (psychographics), and are located near the camp operation. Additionally, because of the larger, more generic target markets, recreational camps apply more mainstream promotional tactics.

- Recreational camps' entertainment and instructional elements come from a variety of activities such as arts and crafts, general sports and games, music, entertainment, and educational field trips.

- Recreational camps typically, but not always, have a higher ratio of staff to campers. Safety concerns will determine a recreational camp's philosophy of staff-to-camper ratio.

- Recreational camp staffs consist of a wider variety of child care professionals, who can range from C.I.T.s (counselors in training) to tenured educational instructors and administrators.

- Recreational camps have a wide range of operational facilities. They can vary from basic park space to elaborate community centers and schools. Recreational camps, if government subsidized (e.g., parks and recreation departments), can have extremely low prices and costs. If a recreation camp is with a private organization, the prices and costs can be moderate to very expensive, depending on camp activities and recreational programs.

Instructional Sports Camps

Some components that are typical for an instructional sports camp include the following:

- Instructional sports camps have more focused target markets. While the geographic area varies greatly from camp to camp (local, regional, or national), demographic characteristics and psychographic lifestyles are easier to identify and track due to the common factors of the particular sport.

- Sports camps are instructional based with entertainment activities occasionally added, depending on time constraints and type of camp. Most additional entertainment activities are related to the camp's particular sport.

- Instructional sports camps are associated with sport-specific skill development rather than generic child care.

- Staff-to-camper ratio is based on ideal instruction within a maximum group size. Additionally, it is not unusual to have breakout sessions that have smaller staff-to-camper ratios, some even down to individual, one-on-one instruction.

- Instructional staff consist of sports-specific athletes and professional coaches. The quality of their instruction is a key factor in the success of the operation.

- The operational facilities and equipment are sport specific. Athletic facilities can range from public educational institutions to colleges and universities to private commercial facilities.

- Because of the high operating costs associated with instructional sports camps, prices for them can range from reasonable to extremely high.

ENTREPRENEURIAL VENTURES VERSUS INSTITUTIONAL CAMPS

Entrepreneurial Camps

Entrepreneurs see and try to develop interesting and potentially profitable business opportunities while identifying difficulties and possible pitfalls of those opportunities. They are typically driven by success and have an original outlook on their particular interests and customer needs. An entrepreneur's desire for independence in decision-making must balance with his/her level of risk taking. Simply stated, entrepreneurship often has big payoffs with high levels of risk. It is not for the faint of heart.

Entrepreneurial summer sports camps take on the same elements as any other business. They strive for

- a competitive advantage in the marketplace. Sustainable competitive advantage is characterized as when a company can "meet customer needs more effectively or efficiently than rivals and when the basis for this is durable, despite the best efforts of competitors to match or surpass this advantage[7]";

- customer satisfaction through model service;

- profitability and sound financial performance; and

- strong strategic alliances, community goodwill, and a distinct market presence.

An entrepreneur's greatest motivation is for profit and increased wealth. Is this goal contrary to providing a quality instructional camp experience for all participants? Absolutely not. In fact, for entrepreneurial ventures to survive, they have to routinely provide higher quality than institutional ventures. Institutions often have brand insistence because of their size and reputation; entrepreneurs need to work hard to develop theirs.

Institutional Camps

Institutional sports camps are customarily associated with educational organizations such as local junior or senior high schools and colleges and universities. While institutional camps prioritize sound business goals, competitive advantage, customer service, etc., their working objectives typically benefit the athletic program, a particular team within the athletic department, and internal and external participants of the program or team. In comparison to entrepreneurial camps, which have freedom and independence, institutional camps customarily have considerably more contractual agreements, restrictions, and regulations. Prior to developing and operating an institutional camp, answer the following questions:

1. What types of rules and regulations do the athletic program's governing body have regarding institutional sport instruction camps? The program's governing body might include organizations such as local and state high school athletic associations, NJCAA, NCAA, or the NAIA. Are there regulations on the number of contact hours, coaches' involvement, recruiting, and financial reporting? If so, will these rules negatively impact operations and ultimately affect the success of the camp?

2. Are there specific institutional rules and regulations that could impact the camp? For instance, are there restrictions on facility and equipment usage, maintenance, safety, or parking? Will the sports camp require budget approval by the institution? Will the institution require marketing and promotional approval?

3. What are the financial arrangements and contractual requirements the camp operation has with the institution? What is the basis for these financial arrangements? Is there an established per-camper percentage to be paid to the institution? Is there a predetermined cost structure with upfront rental fees, maintenance costs, auxiliary services, etc.?

4. Will the sports camp be an individual camp or a cooperative, combined element of the athletic department's summer camp program? If a component of an umbrella camp program, what arrangement and position will the individual sports camp occupy? Within the athletic program's summer camp, what are the administrative and managerial reporting responsibilities? How will the individual summer sports camps be prioritized within the combined make-up?

DAY CAMPS VERSUS OVERNIGHT CAMPS

The decision of whether to run a daytime summer sports camp (transient) or an overnight sports camp (residential) is far-reaching and significant. One must consider logistical operations, revenue streams, human resource needs, ancillary services, and expenses/profitability.

Day camps (in which camp athletes come for specific hours during the day/evening and then return home) have numerous advantages and disadvantages compared to overnight/stay-away camps. The advantages of day camp usually include

- less financial risk and overall costs,
- reduced administrative headaches, and
- instructional staff focused on teaching rather than overnight camp responsibilities.

The most obvious disadvantage is the camp's limited geographic area. Because campers are being dropped off and picked up after every session, only campers in a limited geographic area can attend. If a day camp is being held in a densely populated location, this concern could be moot. However, if a summer instructional camp's location is in a rural, sparsely populated area, a day camp model might be difficult or unrealistic. Time constraints can also be disadvantages to day camps. Because of transportation issues, session times must be strictly observed. Finally, logistical matters such as safe pick-up and drop-off areas, daily parking, and parental observation areas are just some of the issues that need to be addressed.

An overnight sports camp's immediate advantage over day camps relates to its ability to attract youth athletes outside a specific geographic area. In theory, a prestigious summer sports camp that is well known could draw attendees from all areas of the country and beyond. Another important advantage for overnight camps is that they traditionally have more scheduling flexibility because they have significantly more time to plan sessions and activities throughout multiple days and nights. Overnight camps also have numerous revenue streams that can add to the profitability of the camp. Unfortunately, along with the increased number of revenue streams comes an increase in costs. The disadvantages and concerns with running an overnight instructional camp can be considerable. The immediate disadvantage will be the drastically increased administrative work involved with operating an overnight camp. Organizational difficulties such as coordinating housing, food services, and

Camp Tip

The primary difference between an entrepreneurial summer sports camp and institutional camp lies in risk. Entrepreneurial camps have tremendous financial upsides; however (and unfortunately), the individual owners can also experience substantial financial losses. Conversely, institutional camps often have limitations on the financial gains by the individual operators, but fortunately, financial losses can be absorbed by the institution rather than the individuals involved in their operation.

supplementary activities come into play. Overnight camps have additional liability and safety issues that go beyond normal camp training issues. Simply stated, from the second a camp starts, an overnight camp is responsible 24 hours a day for each individual camper. This can be daunting. With that said, the increase in instructional staff's roles and responsibilities will frequently go beyond sport instruction to child care and safety.

ENDNOTES

1. Byars, L. L., & Rue, L. W. (2011). *Human resource management* (10th edition), p. 234. New York, NY: McGraw-Hill/Irwin.
2. Jones, G. R., & George, J. M. (2004). *Essentials of contemporary management,* p. 281. New York, NY: McGraw-Hill/Irwin.
3. Perreault, W. D., Cannon, J. P., & McCarthy, E. J. (2012). *Essentials of marketing* (13th edition), p. 200. New York, NY: McGraw-Hill/Irwin.
4. Scarborough, N. M. (2011). *Essentials of entrepreneurship and small business management* (6th edition), p. 3. Upper Saddle River, NJ: Prentice Hall.
5. Longenecker, J. G., Moore, C. W., & Petty, J. W. (2003). *Small business management: An entrepreneurial emphasis* (12th edition), p. 11. Mason, OH: Thompson Southwestern.
6. Byrd, M. J., & Megginson, L. C. (2009). *Small business management: An entrepreneur's guidebook* (6th edition), p. 325. New York, NY: McGraw-Hill/Irwin.
7. Thompson, A. A., Peteraf, M. A., Gamble, J. E., & Strickland, A. J. (2012). *Crafting and executing strategy: The quest of competitive advantage* (18th edition), p. 5. New York, NY: McGraw Hill/Irwin.

2

Conducting a Feasibility Study

CONDUCTING A FEASIBILITY STUDY

In their 2014 text, *Entrepreneurial Small Business,* Katz and Green define feasibility studies as "the extent to which an idea is viable and realistic and the extent to which you are aware of internal (to your business) and external (industry, market, and regulatory environment) forces that could affect your business." They go on to say that "feasibility studies consist of careful investigation of five primary areas: the overall business idea, the product and service, the industry and market, financial projections (profitability), and the plan for future actions."[1] Up to now, this book has examined the overall business idea and the product and service associated with a summer sports camp. To examine the industry and market, profitability, and future plans, which are essential in deciding whether or not to operate a summer sports camp, the following tools should be used:

1. An external analysis that scans the primary external macroenvironmental factors

2. The Five Forces Model of Competition

3. An outline of the key success factors involved in an instructional sports camp

4. A SWOT (strengths, weaknesses, opportunities, threats) review

Macroenvironmental Factors

The external environmental factors that must be scanned during a feasibility study for a summer sports camp are technology, nature, social, economic, political/legal, and demographic. These considerations will affect how the camp instruction is perceived, accepted, and desired by the target market.

Technology

The first environmental factor one should examine is technology. A no-nonsense definition of technology that applies to summer camp operations is "the practical implementation of learning and knowledge by individuals and organizations to aid human endeavors. Technology is the knowledge, products, processes, tools, and systems used in the creation of goods or in the provision of services."[2] To look at technology as an environmental factor, one must determine which current or future technological advance could benefit the camp and which could hurt if not utilized.

There are virtually no businesses (and camp operations are businesses) that are not greatly affected by the accelerating pace of technological change. Computerization, cell phones, advanced training systems, social media, and the Internet are just a small number of technological advances that need to be considered. The technological review should focus not only on currently available technology but also on projected technological advances that might affect the camp's future. Some questions to ask when conducting external research into technology include the following:

- From our research, are our current system capabilities, even though they might be manual, economical and practical? In the future, will this put our operation at a disadvantage?

- Are there technology systems (hardware and software) available that could increase camp efficiency? What will be the immediate monetary outlay? Will there be long-term cost savings and competitive advantages from these systems?

- Is there generic software that can be adapted to the potential operation or would camp-specific software systems be more practical? What are the cost differences?

- What is the learning curve for new technological advancements? Will the time spent learning new technology be the best use of the camp's human resources?

- What type of use can technology be in marketing communication? How important are web pages, social media, email blasts, and various e-publications and e-brochures for the camp operation? Do we have the internal abilities to develop these?

- Are there technological advances in training the particular sport? If so, are they practical to develop for a new operation? If these training technologies are considered essential, can the new camp afford to learn and develop them?

Camp Tip

Not all technological improvements are right for all would-be camps. One must balance cost with necessity. If a camp administrator finds that a necessary technology component cannot be acquired, he or she might consider not operating the camp.

These are just some of the questions that need to be investigated when looking at technology.

Nature Factors

For most camps, the natural environment is as significant an environmental factor as any other external factor. Obviously, outdoors sports programs need to address weather patterns, pollution, and other possible natural concerns that could influence camp activities. For example, from a scheduling standpoint, one might find that the only times an outdoor camp facility is unoccupied are in the afternoon. In most parts of this country, outdoor camp sessions in the summer are a serious medical concern for camp participants and clinicians. If afternoon is the only available time, one should consider not holding the camp. Even if a summer camp is primarily indoors, nature and weather can still affect camp operations. Know the area's natural elements in which you want to run a summer sport camps and be aware of any potential hazards.

Social

Social environmental elements

> affect how and why people live and behave as they do—which affects customer buying behaviors and eventually economic, political, and legal environments. Many variables make up the cultural and social environment. Some examples are the languages people speak; the type of education they have; their religious beliefs; what type of food they eat; the style of clothing and housing they have; and how they view work, marriage, and family.[3]

Based on this definition, the leading questions that surface for summer sports camp programs include:

1. How does society view our sport and athletic organization? Does this viewpoint impact our camp?

2. What marketing opportunities are possible from the sport's societal attitude? Does the sport have an identifiable target market within our operational area?

3. Are some subcultures more interested in our sport and camp program than others? If so, can these groups be a primary focus within our area of operation?

4. Does society expect the athletic organization and summer sports camp to act in a socially responsible way?

5. Will any of the listed societal variables (detailed earlier) be obstacles in our operation of a summer sports camp? If so, can they be overcome or do they threaten our camp?

To investigate societal factors that may or may not affect a camp, one needs to examine data as well as opinions to determine if these factors will influence a potential operation. Numerical data for the potential target markets can comprise selective demographic information (real characteristics) such as income, education, and percentages of participation in sports. Opinion-based information can be derived from informed discussions with local individuals as well as other athletic program administrators.

Economic

The economic environment refers to purchasing power and unrestricted income (also known as *discretionary income*) in a region. An economic environment that is stable or growing has stronger purchasing power. The stronger the purchasing power, the higher the discretionary spending. This presents numerous market opportunities for a summer sports camp. Conversely, the more financially depressed the economic situation, the less the purchasing power and flexible spending. A climate of economic downturn and recession presents a significant concern for a camp whose foundation is based on unconstrained and flexible spending.

Knowing that athletes, coaches, and camp administrators are not economists, the best way to examine the economic environment is to look at the following three sources:

- Unemployment: One main indicator of economic health is the unemployment rate. To find the national, state, and local unemployment rates, look at the Bureau of Labor Statistics (www.bls.gov) to provide all the meaningful facts and measurements of critical employment data.

- Personal Income: Another vital gauge for an economic review is to examine personal income and its corresponding flexible or discretionary spending. To find the national, state, and local personal income statistics, the Bureau of Economic Analysis is the most reliable source (www.bea.gov).

- Economic Experts: The final resource that will determine the economic feasibility of a summer sports camp is the use of experts in determining the camp's practicality. These professionals are economic specialists who explain monetary trends and economic forecasts and then communicate this information through various publications. Information from these individuals can be retrieved from assorted national, state, and local business and economics journals.

Camp Tip

When considering using expert data, the most valuable retrieval source will be librarians. Their expertise at gathering and sorting information is incredible. To utilize them, know what information is needed, when it is needed, and how it will be used. This, in turn, will focus their assistance and provide you with target data that will support one's decisions. (In our case, do economic conditions reveal whether to run a summer sports camp or not?)

CHAPTER 2

Political/Legal

The political/legal factor in environmental scanning is the legislation affecting one's summer sports camp. From a sports standpoint, summer camps have three tiers of legislation to identify and monitor. The first is U.S. governmental legislation that all businesses have to recognize and with which they must comply. Examples of this can range from the Internal Revenue Service (IRS) to the Immigration and Naturalization Service to the Equal Employment Opportunity Commission. The second tier is the particular sport's governing body and its guiding rules and bylaws. The concentration and intensity of regulations, bylaws, and directives is sport specific as well as level specific (e.g., NCAA, NAIA, high school athletic associations). The final tier is the particular institution's rules and regulations (if applicable).

To find relevant regulatory information for these three tiers, it is important to understand what information is appropriate to your particular situation and to be familiar with basic internet research techniques. For U.S. governmental information, consulting with lawyers who can assist with all human resource concerns and Certified Public Accountants (CPAs) who can determine all financial reporting requirements would be sensible. For the particular sport's governing body, online manuals and phone hotlines are readily available. Finally, for one's identifiable institution, policy and procedure manuals as well as direct contact with athletic program administrators should be easily accessible. No matter which legislative tier one is investigating, it is a wise move to document each interaction and decision.

© Rambleon | Dreamstime.com

If, for any reason, the legal and regulatory requirements for a camp become a drain or obstacle to one's potential operation, then reconsider the practicality of operating the camp. Could this happen? Without question—yes. A camp administrator must record all possible regulatory compliance concerns, preferably in order of compliance importance, and review each for its feasibility and burden on the potential camp's goals and management.

Demographic

The final external element to survey relates to the demographic characteristics of both the overall market and the camp's target market segment. *Demographics* is defined as

> the distribution of individuals in a society in terms of age, sex, marital status, income, ethnicity, and other personal attributes that may determine buying patterns. Understanding this basic information about a population can help a firm determine whether its products or services will appeal

to customers and how many potential customers for these products or services it might have.[4]

Demographics are the concrete characteristics of individuals who make up the camp's target market profile. With this information, camps can concentrate sometimes limited resources directly on clear-cut customer groups. Demographic knowledge can help predict the best course of action for reaching future potential customers. Simply put, customers change. By knowing current customers, an administrator can forecast what they will be like in the future.

Demographic shifts can have a tremendous impact on whether to run a summer sports camp or to reconsider its practicality. To discover demographic shifts, one will need to examine trends in the camp's geographic area. For example, what are the expected growth rates and demographic changes in the area? What have the past five years of demographic data shown? Is the community becoming older? Are there more families moving into the area? What are the professional backgrounds of current and future residents? These are just a few of the questions that need to be answered when discussing the demographic environmental factor.

Five Forces Model of Competition

When performing a feasibility study for a prospective summer sports camp, the most far-reaching and consequential element to consider is competition. As one of the country's foremost theorists in strategic management, Michael E. Porter has numerous models and theories that can be applied to analyzing the competitive environment. One of his most universally known concepts is the Five Forces Model, which probes an industry's principal external competitive components:

Forces Governing Competition in an Industry: Five Forces Model

- Threat of new entrants

- Bargaining power of suppliers

- Threat of substitute products or services

- Bargaining power of customers

- The industry: Jockeying for position among current competition[5]

The Five Forces Model delves into the external competitive components in an industry, the summer sports camp industry, in this case. In order to use the Five Forces Model, camp administrators must take the wide-ranging categories given by Porter and focus them on their potential camp operations. Additionally, before elaborating on each individual factor of the model, it must be stated that the more influence the force has on potential camp operations, the more of a danger and serious consideration it is. Conversely, the more influence the potential camp has on the force, the more possibility exists for exploiting new opportunities.

Camp Tip

To shape the Five Forces Model components, a new summer sports camp must have strong core competencies. Core competencies are the internal abilities, skills, resources, and talents of the organization. Simply put, to control the external elements, one should have a strong internal foundation. If these are immediately unattainable, strong consideration should be given to developing them and postponing a camp's introduction.

New Camp Entrants

The first element in Porter's concept that can be adapted to sports camps is the examination of potential new competitors entering the competitive environment. In other words, who has the capability to enter the competitive environment and what do they offer? New entrants can be start-up camp programs with no prior history, or they can be from established athletic organizations trying to expand into different arenas. By far, this category is the most difficult to predict. Suppliers, buyers, competitive rivalry, and substitutes are already existing components that are tangible in nature and grounded in reality. New entrants require more guesswork because of uncertainty.

> In investigating this classification of the model, one needs to comprehend the expected reaction of incumbent firms to new entry and what are known as barriers to entry. Industry incumbents that are willing and able to launch strong defensive maneuvers to maintain their position can make it hard for a new entrant to gain a sufficient market foothold to survive and eventually become profitable. . . . [A] barrier to entry exists whenever it is hard for a newcomer to break into the market and/or the economics of the business put a potential entrant at a disadvantage.[6]

Simply stated, the stronger the reaction from existing camps and the higher the barriers, the more difficult it would be for a new camp to break into the competitive environment. The opposite is also true. The weaker the response from current camps and the lower the barriers, the more of a danger a new entrant can be to an established camp. To dissect this section of the model, look at all of the barriers to entry, then recognize who could fulfill these barrier requirements, then finally determine if they will enter the competitive environment.

Power of Suppliers

The second external segment that needs to be analyzed is the bargaining power of suppliers. Clearly stated, suppliers furnish the inputs for an organization's outputs. In adapting this to sports camps, the output is the quality of the instruction and the skill advancement of the camp athletes. What are some of the inputs the camp must have to produce those output? Administrative personnel, former and current athletes, former and current coaches and clinicians, specialized facilities and equipment, and sponsorships and apparel are just a few of the supplier concerns to address.

Camp Tip

In almost every athletic organization and sport, athletic programs and their potential summer sports camp operations are divided into levels or tiers. If one's potential camp is classified as tier one, a high-profile athletic organization that has a commanding history of achievement and exposure, the administrators can usually control the relationship with the suppliers. However, if one's athletic program is lower tier and not as high profile, with limited funding and little or no brand recognition, dealing with suppliers requires an altogether different approach. Simply stated, the suppliers control the relationship. Analyze all of the inputs into the potential summer sports camp and formulate the input strategies from there.

Substitutes

The concept of substitutes relates to the ease and availability of other products and services that the consumer can use instead of the organization's product or service. In the case of summer sports camps, this competitive force can be a sizable concern. As discussed, a camp in a particular sport has to compete not only with similar camps in the same sport but also with other sports camps in different sports. Additionally, another substitute could be recreational camps that have nothing to do with athletics. Finally, because this service deals with flexible, discretionary spending, a substitute could be having children stay at home with no summer camp experience.

If one's camp is located in a region where there are a limited number of sports camps and summer child care programs, then direct substitutes would be less of a threat to the potential operation's customer base. On the other hand, if one's camp is located in an area with ample substitute camps and summer child care programs, customer support would be uncertain, as would interest and camp publicity. To distinguish all of the possible substitutes to the camp, list all of the key components of the camp program, rank them and examine each one for the danger of substitutes. The more meaningful and significant the ingredient of the summer sports camp, the more the administrator will need specific actions to minimize the effects of any possible substitutes. If one realizes that the market is overloaded with substitutes, each potential alternative will need to be examined as to its particular threat to the prospective camp.

Bargaining Power of Buyers

Camp Tip

Once again, if the athletic program or organization is first tier, and has a high profile and solid track record, camp demand and sales are a distinct opportunity. If the athletic program is lower tiered, finding potential campers could be a major summer sports camp threat. In this situation, one's method of gaining customers would, in most cases, need to be inventive and continuous.

This exterior factor relates to customers and their demand for one's particular sports camp instruction. The more in demand one's camp, the more power one has over customers. Unfortunately, the reverse is also true. This is tricky for new camps because demand is undetermined and cannot be verified. For a feasibility study, it is imperative that some type of research be conducted that looks at the potential customers' demand for one's camp. The research needs to examine customer factors such as knowledge of the camp, current camp purchases and willingness to switch, price sensitivity, service and quality expectations, importance placed on sport and skill development, and overall impression of the camp operation. The research could be through surveys, focus groups, informal discussions, or a combination of all of these. This data will establish the power of the buyers and whether it is realistic to acquire them for one's new venture.

Rivalry Among Existing Camps

This classification is the most recognizable of the Five Forces Model. The camp's immediate competition is the one strategic element of which potential administrators tend to be mindful without needing to be reminded. The camp's output and results are a direct reflection of its competitors' output and results. The stronger the competitors, the more of a threat they are. Before launching a new camp, closely examine the "competitive battlefield" the camp is entering. To get a true picture of the competitive intensity in the market, the following factors need to be scrutinized:

- number of direct and indirect competitors;
- history, mission, culture, and reputation of each competitor's athletic program and summer sports camp;
- size and scope of competitor's operations;
- marketing communication tactics used by competitors;
- key strategic alliances each competitor has developed;
- current position of each competitor in the overall market, referred to as the market share;
- the resources competitors have access to, such as facilities, equipment, and all other noteworthy assets;
- human resource capabilities and skills of competing camps, especially in administrative and clinical instruction;
- internal operational efficiency of competition in terms of systems and technology;
- price structure of competitors' camps; and
- other unique elements that make each competitor distinctive.

Key Success Factors

Key success factors are

> the factors that determine a company's ability to compete successfully in an industry. Every company in an industry must understand the key success factors driving the industry; otherwise they are likely to become industry "also-rans" like the horses trailing the pack in the Kentucky Derby.[7]

Key success factors for summer sport camps programs are current and future elements that are universally critical for all summer sports camp programs. For example, it is this book's fundamental premise that all camp administrators need strong administrative capabilities. Administrative talent would be a universal key success factor for all summer sports camps. For a feasibility study, an administrator and personnel should, through firsthand observations and experience, examine the summer sports camp industry's key success factors and then look at their potential camp program with these in mind. Simply stated, once the camp's key success factors have been clarified, a camp administrator needs to do the following:

- Evaluate how the potential sports camp and industry key success factors match up. Does the prospective camp program rate stronger, weaker, or the same in industry key success factors? The camp's standing in these areas will have far-reaching effects on whether or not to operate the camp currently and in the future.
- Compare how the camp's potential competition is doing in relation to the industry-wide key success factors.

Camp Tip

When analyzing the competitive intensity (using the points listed), it is important to have a blend of opinions along with measurable data. The more hard data and reliable information collected, the clearer the picture of the intensity of competitive rivalry. This information is essential for deciding whether to jump into a summer sports camp operation or to postpone market penetration until one's internal capabilities and resources are sufficient to handle the current competition.

- Analyze current key success factors for their future increasing or diminishing importance.
- Project possible future driving forces in summer sports camps and lay the groundwork on how to confront them. Driving forces can be such factors as public perceptions of the potential camp operation, increase or reduction of the overall athletic program's popularity, levels of the governing body rules and regulatory authority, and individual sport improvements such as training techniques, administrative methods, and camp management.

Some key success factors for the summer camp industry are delineated in Table 2.1.

Camp Tip

It should be noted that on top of the key success factors that all camps must identify and strategize for, each individual sport will have its own unique key success factors to define and address.

Table 2.1. **Universal Key Success Factors for Summer Sports Camps**

Quality of Instruction	Administrative Competence
Price and Value	Customer Service
Status and Public Identity	Technology Expertise
Location and Accessibility	Facilities and Equipment
Resources and Assets	Strategic Alliances
Market Share	Culture and Ethical Philosophy
Accommodations	Food Service
Supplier Relationship	Regulatory Compliance
Product Selection (General versus Specialty Instruction)	

SWOT Analysis

Another core tool in judging a camp's potential development is from an internal and external perspective. This is the foundation of a SWOT analysis (strengths, weaknesses, opportunities, threats). Internally, one needs to perform a strength and weakness study. Very similar to a pro and con assessment, an internal strength and weakness evaluation looks critically at all possible internal camp factors. The key word is *critically*. Consider every aspect of the potential camp and consider whether it is a strength (asset) or a weakness (liability). It is advisable to start the strength/weakness review by prioritizing the factors of the camp's operation from most necessary to least important. Hopefully, when the evaluation is completed, the most significant operational elements will be considered strengths. A camp administrator's philosophy in converting the internal analysis to strategizing should be to always maximize strengths and minimize weaknesses (or even convert the weaknesses to strengths).

Clearly, the business does not have to correct all its weaknesses, nor should it gloat about all of its strengths. The big question is whether the business should limit itself to those opportunities where it possesses the required strength or whether it should consider better opportunities where it might have to acquire or develop certain strengths.[8]

If the strengths are overwhelmingly in favor of camp development, then one should strongly consider its launch. Regrettably, if the analysis points to major core weaknesses that cannot be overcome, then one will need to consider passing on the venture.

The second step when exploring the possible launch of a new camp is an external analysis or an opportunity/threat study. This process examines the external environmental factors that affect the camp's operation to determine if they are threats to the camp or possibilities for growth and competitive advantage. Items such as the macroenvironmental factors (discussed earlier in this section) as well as market size and potential, direct and indirect competitors, and athletic advancements are all important to analyze. Once again, prioritize the environmental elements from the most significant to the least notable. If one is fortunate, opportunities will outweigh threats. The camp administrator's goal should be to exploit opportunities and fortify the camp against threats. If the opportunities are greater than threats, then the situation may be right to launch a camp. If threats outweigh opportunities, the potential camp may need to be re-evaluated.

Once management has identified the major threats and opportunities facing a specific business unit, it can characterize that business's overall attractiveness. Four outcomes are possible:

- An ideal business is high in major opportunities and low in major threats.
- A speculative business is high in both major opportunities and threats.
- A mature business is low in major opportunities and low in threats.
- A troubled business is low in opportunities and high in threats.[9]

To strategize from the strengths/weaknesses and opportunities/threats stage is straightforward logic. The best-case scenario is that the potential camp has a distinct strength that can be used to exploit an external opportunity. At the other end of the

---

Strength-------------Opportunity
Take advantage of one's superiority and exploit the opportunity.
Strength-------------Threat
In this scenario, the camp should be able to neutralize this danger.
Weakness------------Opportunity
This condition needs a resolution. Does the camp strengthen the weakness to take advantage of the circumstance or does it pass on the opportunity? Remember, this dilemma is potentially dangerous. If the camp passes on the opportunity and the program's competition takes advantage of the situation, it might then become a distinct threat.
Weakness------------Threat
This condition typically requires a prompt action to be taken. The more hazardous and powerful the threat, the more immediate and decisive the need to respond to it.

Figure 2.1. **SWOT Scenario Analysis**

Camp Tip

Another way to look at a SWOT analysis is to maximize the potential camp's internal strengths, minimize its internal weaknesses, exploit its external opportunities, and defend against its external threats.

---

spectrum, the camp might have a weakness that coincides with an external threat. As the administrator, one should look at each external element as it relates to the internal operational strengths/weaknesses. There are four primary scenarios (see Figure 2.1).

CAMP THEME AND OPERATIONAL STRATEGY

To develop and operate a camp, the camp administrator needs to determine the theme and the camp's overall strategy. There are five themes, or broad competitive strategies, that must be examined by any business operation.

1. A low-cost provider strategy: striving to achieve lower overall costs than rivals on products that attract a broad spectrum of buyers.

2. A broad differentiation strategy: differentiating the company's product offering from the competition with attributes that appeal to a broad spectrum of buyers.

3. A focused, or market niche, low-cost strategy: concentrating on a narrow buyer segment and outcompeting rivals on costs, thus being in position to win buyer favor with lower-priced product offerings.

4. A focused, or market niche, differentiation strategy: concentrating on a narrow buyer segment and outcompeting rivals with a product offering that meets the specific tastes and requirements of niche members better than the product offerings of rivals.

5. A best-cost provider strategy: giving customers more value for the money by offering upscale product attributes at a lower cost than rivals. Being the best-cost producer of an upscale product allows a company to underprice rivals whose products have similar upscale attributes. This option is a hybrid strategy that blends elements of differentiation and low-cost strategies in a unique way.[10]

© Scaliger | Dreamstime.com

A far-reaching camp theme or competitive strategy should not be settled on hastily. It is the foundation of the camp from which all other strategies stem. Once the camp's overall strategy is chosen—and one has to be definitively selected—the camp will be identified and often locked in with that theme in the customer's mind.

No matter what theme and strategy the camp adopts, understand that "most summer camps share a common goal: to bring together new faces, offer new activities, and provide a home-away-from-home experience that helps kids build confidence."[11] While profitability and sports instruction are important objectives of a summer sports camp, the experiences gained by the participants are as important for the camp's future growth and fruition.

ENDNOTES

1. Katz, J., & Green, R. (2014). *Entrepreneurial small business* (4th edition), p. 94. New York, NY: McGraw-Hill/Irwin.

2. White, M. A., & Bruton, G. D. (2007). *The management of technology and innovation: A strategic approach*, p. 16. Mason, OH: Thompson South-Western.

3. Perreault, W. D., Cannon, J. P., & McCarthy, E. J. (2012). *Essentials of marketing* (13th edition), p. 71. New York, NY: McGraw-Hill/Irwin.

4. Barney, J. B., & Hesterly, W. S. (2012). *Strategic management and competitive advantage: Concepts and cases* (4th edition), p. 31. Upper Saddle River, NJ: Pearson Education.

5. Porter, M. E. (1998). *On competition*, p. 22. Boston, MA: Harvard Business Review Books.

6. Thompson, A. A., Peteraf, M. A., Gamble, J. E., & Strickland, A. J. (2014). *Crafting and executing strategy: The quest of competitive advantage* (19th edition), p. 54. New York, NY: McGraw Hill/Irwin.

7. Scarborough, N. M. (2011). *Essentials of entrepreneurship and small business management* (6th edition), p. 80. Upper Saddle River, NJ: Prentice Hall.

8. Kotler, P. (2003). *Marketing management* (11th edition), p. 104. Upper Saddle River, NJ: Prentice Hall.

9. Kotler, P. (2003). *Marketing management* (11th edition), p. 104. Upper Saddle River, NJ: Prentice Hall.

10. Thompson, A. A., Peteraf, M. A., Gamble, J. E., & Strickland, A. J. (2014). *Crafting and executing strategy: The quest of competitive advantage* (19th edition), pp. 121-122. New York, NY: McGraw Hill/Irwin.

11. Howard, A. W., & Moore, C. J. (2008). Nonprofit summer camps offer kids much more than s'mores. *The Chronicle of Philanthropy, 20*, 1

SECTION II:

PLANNING

There are clear benefits and uses associated with creating a camp plan. The most important are furnishing internal and external participants with focus for the future; projecting professionalism to external groups and individuals; giving administrators, clinicians, and staff members a sense of stability and teamwork; and providing the operation with a strong foundation. In other words, it simply determines what can or cannot be accomplished.

The camp plan is not a stagnant document. It should be considered a flexible camp element that needs constant updates and improvements. While most revisions will be minor, they are crucial in maintaining the plan's ongoing benefits. The ability to adapt and amend the camp plan to the changing environment could mean the difference between a camp's success or breakdown.

3

Planning Overview

INTRODUCTION: WHY CONSTRUCT A SUMMER SPORTS CAMP PLAN?

Because of the short-term nature of camp operations, one might reasonably ask why camp administrators should compose a plan for an organization that will only exist for a few weeks. While on the surface this concern has merit, a camp plan can have astonishing benefits for the camp organization as well as for the individuals employed in its development, implementation, and management. Will the camp plan require time to create and refine into a working document? Most definitely. As this section will show, it will be time well spent.

© Anatols | Dreamstime.com

The following are central reasons to devote additional time and energy to the generation of a sound camp plan.

1. A summer sports camp plan furnishes participants with an analytical, commonsense structure for making decisions. Camp decisions should always be

   > made on the strength of the underlying business idea, but it is much easier to come to a decision if the idea is communicated simply and clearly in a well-written business plan. The discipline required to articulate the business strategy, tactics, and operations in a written document ensures rigorous analysis and greater clarity of thought.[1]

   With that said, it is likely that a summer sports camp plan will help significantly in making reasonable decisions (either pre-camp, during camp, or post-camp). This, in turn, will reduce potential resource waste, personnel confusion, operational risk, and public relation issues.

2. A comprehensive camp plan will provide the operation with a well-defined vision for the future and a clear structure for all camp participants. A vision is "an ideal and unique image of the future. The vision enlists the emotions of group members and points them toward coordinated efforts. The vision binds members through a shared emotional commitment."[2] This emotional commitment could very well be the difference between a good camp and a great one that surpasses everyone's expectations.

3. Essential benefits associated with the development and execution of a strong camp plan are the real increases in internal efficiency and the quality of the output and services. Efficiency is best described as using fewer camp inputs to make a quality camp output/service. The vital word is *quality*. It is easy to use less input (money, labor, assets, etc.) to produce a second-rate output or service. A camp plan can help ensure an effective use of inputs while maintaining (and, in some cases, boosting) the quality of the camp's output or service. From a financial perspective, the more internally efficient the camp, the more its profit margin increases.

4. Depending on numerous factors, such as geographic area, sport, rivalry of established camps, years in operation, and reputation and image of camp and coaches, a thorough camp plan can help develop a sustained competitive advantage over current and potential competitors. Competitive advantage can be founded on several factors, but the ultimate determination is in the camp's profitability and durability.

With well-presented and rational strategies, a sound camp plan can unquestionably contribute to those outcomes. Additionally, not only does a sound plan organize a competitive strategy for the camp to follow, it can help establish counterstrategies and strategic answers to the tactics of direct and indirect competitors.

5. A skillfully written camp plan promotes clear lines of internal communication rather than the often uncontrollable informal channels known as the "grapevine." In most organizations, the grapevine "usually carries far more information than the formal communication system, and on many matters it is more effective in determining the course for an organization."[3] The grapevine cannot be eliminated or disregarded. It will always be present in nearly every organization. For a camp administrator who is extremely invested in the camp's operations, it is critical to control the informal grapevine as much as possible. The most important control element is a camp plan that is understandable and reviewed with all administrators, clinicians, and staff. The plan establishes formal communication channels and highlights the significance of each individual in those channels. Furthermore, more emphasis on formal channels can increase benefits such as cooperation, citizenship, teamwork, and loyalty.

6. A sound camp plan creates an atmosphere of professionalism and powerful leadership. This atmosphere (also known as *corporate culture*) legitimizes the camp to all internal and external stakeholders. The importance of professionalism in a camp's operations cannot be overestimated. Professionalism makes a sincere statement to all employees, no matter what their position and responsibilities, that the operation will have the highest standards and behavioral expectations. Professionalism shows parents and campers that this enterprise is first class and dedicated to making a constructive impact on young athletes' lives through an excellent organization and instruction.

7. The two primary ways to increase an organization's net profits are to (1) enlarge revenues and revenue sources and/or (2) control costs and expenses. A sports camp plan can have a sizable impact on resource allocation and cost controls. Resource allocation relates to any organizational component that could be categorized as an asset. For a camp, these would typically consist of money, human resources, equipment, facilities, merchandise, etc. To minimize asset waste or ensure enough assets to distribute and operate the camp, a well-designed camp plan can objectively study asset allocation.

Camp Tip

Planning is not without its obstacles. Developing a camp plan takes time, energy, and critical thought. Camp plans should be considered living documents that need constant attention. Most importantly, planning often deals with uncertainty and making difficult choices. Even with these factors, a camp plan's benefits far outweigh any potential drawbacks.

FOUNDATIONS OF STRATEGIC PLANNING

Before the creation of a camp plan, one will need to know the fundamentals of the overall strategic management process. In the text *Essentials of Entrepreneurship and Small Business Management,* Norman Scarborough lays out nine steps in the strategic management process:

Step 1: Develop a clear vision and translate it into a meaningful mission statement.

Step 2: Assess the company's strengths and weaknesses.

Step 3: Scan the environment for significant opportunities and threats facing the business.

Step 4: Identify the key factors for success in the business.

Step 5: Analyze the competition.

Step 6: Create goals and objectives.

Step 7: Formulate strategic options and select the appropriate strategies.

Step 8: Translate strategic plans into action plans.

Step 9: Establish accurate controls.[4]

While many of these steps were accomplished during the camp's feasibility study (discussed in Chapter 2), as the following section will demonstrate, they will be the foundation of the fully functional camp plan.

Type of Plan

The camp administrator must spell out, well in advance of construction, which type of plan is the most applicable for the venture.

> The business plan itself varies with the type of organization, the type of goals being set, and the scope of the plan in terms of time and overall coverage. Plans vary with the stage of the firm's development with respect to the plan's focus and content.[5]

The questions that need to be answered relate to two fundamental areas of planning:

1. Will the camp employ a single-use plan or a permanent standing plan?
2. Will the plan be used for internal operations or for external development and funding?

Single-Use and Standing Plans

"Single-use plans are developed to achieve a set of goals unlikely to be repeated in the future. Standing plans are ongoing plans used to provide guidance for task performance repeated within the organization."[6] In the plainest language, single-use plans are one-time documents for projects that have specific timeframes. Their complexity and purpose depends on the significance assigned to the one-time camp project. For camps, that can range from a brief summary to a detailed step-by-step blueprint of the entire operation. Standing plans are just that: They are plans produced for enterprises that will be ongoing and year to year. Depending on strategic changes, the substance of standing plans can be rolled over from camp to camp and year to year.

© Maigi | Dreamstime.com

Figure 3.1. **Camp Plan Questions**

The remainder of this section will be developed under the assumption that one's summer sports camp operation will be ongoing and will employ standing camp plans.

Internal Operational Plans and External Developmental Plans

The second factor in determining the type of camp plan is whether the document is for internal operations or for external development and funding. This is established by the expected end-users of the camp plan. An internal camp plan furnishes the substance for the entire enterprise and is used by all camp personnel who have duties within the operation. An internal operational camp plan is extremely thorough and focused on every possible component of the summer sports camp. It should be distributed and examined by all internal employees (clinicians, staff, and administrators) and is the source for all current and future actions and functions. In essence, it is the working document where all aspects of the camp originate.

Camp Tip

It is meaningful to note again that standing plans must be considered living documents that need endless evaluation and alterations to stay relevant. It could lead to devastating results if they were considered one-time, in-stone blueprints constructed for multiple years' worth of summer sports camp operations.

An external development camp plan is a summation of the internal plan and is broader based. Its end users can be athletic program executives, financial institutions, community and business leaders, sponsors, etc. The external plan's principal function is for public relations and any outside funding.

A key to connecting the internal and external camp plans is to separate the external plan and complete it *after* the comprehensive internal operational camp plan. The external, by being wide-ranging in scope, summarizes the central highlights for readers who want a short synopsis rather than the nuts and bolts of the operation.

Chapter 4 is developed under the assumption that the camp plan is an internal operational plan.

ENDNOTES

1. Friend, G., & Zehle, S. (2009). *Guide to business planning* (2nd edition), p. 8. New York, NY: Bloomberg Press.

2. Johnson, D. W., & Johnson, F. P. (2006). *Join together: Group theory and group skills* (9th edition), p. 71. Boston, MA: Pearson/Allyn and Bacon.

3. Flatley, M., & Rentz, K. (2010). *Business communication,* p. 11. New York, NY: McGraw-Hill/Irwin.

4. Scarborough, N. M. (2011). *Essentials of entrepreneurship and small business management* (6th edition), pp. 41-42. Upper Saddle River, NJ: Prentice Hall.

5. Truitt, W. (2002). *Business planning: A comprehensive framework and process,* p. 5. Westport, CT: Quorum Books.

6. Draft, R. L., & Marcic, D. (2006). *Understanding management,* p. 169. Mason, OH: Thompson Southwestern.

CHAPTER 4

Components of a Camp Plan

COMPONENTS OF A CAMP PLAN

A camp plan is a direct reflection on the people involved in the organization. For that reason, a camp plan should be a professional presentation that is visually appealing and well written. Professionalism can relate to the look and quality of the paper used, the layout and structure of the document, the cover and title page design, and the characteristics of the binding. Quality writing is not only grammatical with well-structured sentences but includes appropriate wording, content, and brevity. A tightly written and skillfully constructed camp plan emits refinement and competence. A poorly written and disorganized camp plan has a feeling of mismanagement and incompetence.

Table 4.1 is a general outline for a summer sports camp plan (Internal Operational Standing Camp Plan).

Section 1: Vision, Mission, and Value Statements

A sound camp plan begins with three critical statements: (1) vision statement, (2) mission statement, and (3) value statements. Each has its central importance to the operation and the camp plan.

Table 4.1. **Summer Camp Plan Sectional Breakdown**

Section 1: Vision, Mission, and Value Statements

Section 2: Long-Term Objectives and Short-Term Goals

Section 3: SWOT Analysis

Section 4: Operating Systems

Part 1: Human Resource Systems

Part 2: Marketing Systems

Part 3: Financial Systems and Reports

Part 4: Sport Camp Management and Instructional Methodology

Part 5: General Administration/Policies and Procedures

Vision Statement

A camp's vision, which typically projects five-plus years into the future, is more than theoretical appraisal of the camp. Beneficial vision statements are grounded in reality and are written within the reach of the operation.

A clearly defined vision helps a company in four ways:

1. *Vision provides direction.* Entrepreneurs who spell out the vision for their company focus everyone's attention on the future and determine the path the business will take to get there.

2. *Visions determine decisions.* The vision influences the decision, no matter how big or how small, that owners, managers, and employees make every day in a business. This influence can be positive or negative, depending on how well defined the vision is.

3. *Vision motivates people.* A clear vision excites and ignites people to action. People want to work for a company that sets its sights high.

4. *Vision allows for perseverance in the face of adversity.* Young companies, their founders, and their employees often face many hardships from a multitude of sources. Having a vision that serves as a company's "guiding star" enables people to overcome imposing obstacles.[1]

Altogether these points are relevant ingredients in laying the bedrock for a new camp's vision. Conversely, if a camp administrator is drastically modifying the course and vision of an ongoing camp, he or she should acknowledge that some people might resist wholesale vision changes. To help individuals buy into the new vision, it will be important to do the following:

1. Demonstrate to participants the benefit of the new vision.

2. Enlist them in developing the camp's new vision.

3. Reinforce the new vision with convincing and consistent communication.

4. Have a lead-by-example attitude when it comes to the major changes the new vision emphasizes.

Mission Statement

While a vision statement is somewhat abstract, a mission statement links clearly to tangible goals and actions. A mission statement is the all-encompassing message that defines the overall purpose, philosophy, and objectives of the camp operation. "A good mission statement gets people to act in agreement with the company's broader goals. It reminds them how to behave every day regardless of what temporary forces work against them, so that they can help realize the company's vision."[2]

The format and wording used is a matter of individual preference and style. However, when writing the camp's mission statement, answer the following broad questions:

- What is the summer sports camp about?
- What is the summer sports camp's overall purpose?
- What is the philosophy in running the summer sports camp?
- What is the camp's environment?
- What is the current and future status of the summer sports camp?

"The mission is a clear and concise expression of the basic purpose of the organization. It describes what the organization does, who it does it for, its basic good or service, and its values."[3] A camp's mission statement can be as brief as a few sentences or as lengthy as a multi-page explanation. A short, abridged mission statement could be advantageous if the summer sports camp plan is to be utilized for external funding and support. A multi-page statement could be more suitable to motivate internal personnel by providing a detailed foundation and a course of action.

© Rnl | Dreamstime.com

Value Statements

While composing value statements might seem unnecessary, they are invaluable. A strong value statement will define an organization's culture. Consequently,

> if the culture and resulting behavior and work are aligned with the competitive strategies that an organization must execute to win, high performance will result. Culture is also an efficient "gating" mechanism. Much individual behavior can be guided, without supervision, because cultural norm dictates the expected behavior.[4]

Hopefully, these cultural norms will directly originate from and relate to coherent and sound value statements.

Table 4.2. Value Areas to Focus On for a Summer Sports Camp

Campers

The camper experience is everything.

Unconditional commitment to camper safety.

Providing the highest quality clinicians and instructors.

100% participation philosophy for all campers.

Promotion of self-esteem, citizenship, and teamwork.

Employees

Sincerely treated as the most valuable resource in the camp.

Authorized to make decisions.

Trust and support.

Unconditional commitment to staff and clinician safety.

Every person, no matter what the position, is a valuable asset.

Assist in clinician development and training.

Administration

Lead by example: Walk the talk.

Open communication.

Established policies and procedures.

Goal-focused leadership.

Total quality management philosophy in all aspects of the summer sports camp.

©Ladykassie | Dreamstime.com

Section 2: Long-Term Objectives and Short-Term Goals

The next section of the summer sports camp plan deals with distinctive objectives and goals. Long-term objectives are the camp's desires, while short-term goals are a series of explicit actions that will achieve those ambitions.

> A goal, also known as an objective, is a specific commitment to achieve a measurable result within a dated period of time. The goal should be followed by the action plan, which defines the course of action needed to achieve the stated goal.[5]

In actuality, these two components are the central nucleus of the summer sports camp plan. Long-term objectives (three to five years out) will be, to a certain degree, more sizable in their outlook. Short-term goals will be decisive actions that will be used to reach a camp's long-term objectives.

The composition of each objective and goal is up to the camp administrator. However, there are some necessary considerations and guidelines that should be placed on the establishment of goals:

1. All goals should originate from the vision, mission, and values of the camp. If they do not, they can cause internal confusion and a substantial loss of valuable resources and time.

2. When creating goals, long-term objectives should be identified first. Subsequently, short-term actions, which work toward the achievement of each long-term objective, should be created after.

3. It is essential to base all goals in reality. Ask the following questions:
   - Does the camp presently have the resources and capital to achieve its projected goals?
   - Does the camp have the future capability to acquire the vital resources and capital to accomplish the goals?

- Does the camp have the personnel or the likelihood of acquiring the personnel to attain the goals?
- Is the timeframe for the implementation of the camp's goals realistic?
- Will there be any internal or external participant conflicts or resistance to the camp's goals?

4. Camp goals should be understandable by everyone in the organization. They should be uncomplicated, concise, and in common language.

5. Each camp goal should be unique and significant. In other words, are the goals repetitive or are they original?

6. Each camp goal should have the absolute backing and focus of everyone in the organization. In a camp setting, the staff and administrators should be involved in the goal-setting process. Without everyone's input, important personnel might not take an active interest in operations, which, in turn, may leave goals unattained.

7. Each camp objective should be as detailed and measurable as possible. Short-term actions are just that: action-focused tasks that are precise and clear-cut. The advantage of quantifying goals is to supply the camp administrators with concrete numbers so that they can compare projected goals with actual results.

8. Camp goals should be challenging but realistic. Setting goals beyond the reach of current resources and capabilities could be discouraging to camp administrators, clinicians, and staff. Conversely, setting goals that are too easily achieved will devalue the setting and achievement of these goals. A camp administrator must balance these two factors to maximize the camp's potential.

9. In order to be valuable, camp goals need individual and group accountability. Simply put, a camp goal without individual and group accountability will fail because assumptions will be made about who is to work on and accomplish the goal.

10. Camp goals need to be time specific. While the word *deadline* has a negative meaning in our society, it is tremendously appropriate for setting and achieving goals. Once again, the time allotted to achieve a particular camp goal must be challenging but realistic.

In 2009, Leslie Rue and Lloyd Byars outlined 10 possible goal areas that are universal to most businesses in their text, *Management: Skills and Applications*. These 10 areas can be adapted to summer sports camp operations. The following lists those areas.

1. **Profitability**. Measures the degree to which the firm is attaining an acceptable level of profits.

2. **Markets.** Reflects the firm's position in the marketplace.

3. **Productivity.** Measures the efficiency of internal operations.

4. **Product.** Describes the introduction or elimination of products or services.

5. **Financial resources.** Reflects goals relating to the funding needs of the firm.

6. **Physical facilities**. Describes the physical facilities of the firm.

7. **Research and innovation.** Reflects the research, development, or innovation aspirations of the firm.

8. **Organizational structure.** Describes objectives relating to changes in the organizational structure and related activities.

9. **Human resources.** Describes the human resource assets of the organization.

10. **Social responsibility.** Refers to the commitments of the firm regarding society and the environment.[6]

Adapting these 10 areas to a camp's possible goals can include the points illustrated in Table 4.3.

Finally, when constructing goals and objectives, the following are sound tactics to review before and after writing.

One approach to writing objectives that contain these characteristics is to apply a set of criteria to each statement to increase the probability of good objectives. One such list follows:

1. **Relevance.** Are the objectives related to and supportive of the basic purpose of the athletics department?

2. **Practicality.** Do the objectives take into consideration obvious constraints?

3. **Challenge.** Do the objectives provide a challenge?

4. **Measurability.** Are the objectives capable of some form of quantification, if only on an order-of-magnitude basis?

5. **Schedule.** Are the objectives so constituted that they can be time phased and monitored at interim points to ensure progress toward their attainment?

6. **Balance.** Do the objectives provide for a proportional emphasis on all activities and keep the strengths and weaknesses of the organization in proper balance?[7]

Table 4.3. **Potential Goal Areas for Summer Sports Camps:**

Profitability Goals

- Expand Current Target Market Camper Base
- Develop New Possible Summer Sports Camp Markets (expand geographic area, new demographic groups)
- Increase Camp Revenue Sources (additions to product/service lines, e.g., merchandise, individual instruction, etc.)
- Reduce and Control Expenses through Strong Budgeting, Technology Use, and Financial Responsibility (internal resource consumption and operational efficiency)
- Underwriting Expenses through Sponsorships and Strategic Alliances
- Capacity Utilization
- Competitive Advantage Goals: Creating a Sustainable Competitive Advantage over Similar Programs By:
  - Superior Camp Planning and Organizational Structure
  - Strong Operating Systems (administration, marketing, H.R., etc.)
  - Sound Leadership and Camp Management (administration, clinicians, etc.)
  - Well-Known Clinicians and Instructors
  - Quality Control Systems
  - Facility Advantages (new or renovated)

Human Resource Goals

- Objectives to Improve:
  - Acquisition of Administrators, Clinicians, and Staff
  - Camp Orientation Systems (employees and campers)
  - Performance Evaluation Systems
  - Skill, Knowledge, and Attitude Training for All Personnel

Marketing and Promotional Goals

- Creating Awareness for Summer Sports Camp Operation by:
  - Promotion for Increasing Sales
  - Retaining Current Campers
  - Promotion for Community Public Relations

Continuous Improvement Goals

- New Athletic Facilities for Summer Sports Camp Operation
- New Sport Specific Training (for particular sport)
- New Summer Sports Camp Administrative Procedures
- New Legislative Issues (governing bodies)
- New Technological Advances (in camp operations)
- Effective Communication Throughout the Summer Sports Camp
- Resource Utilization and Focus
- Orderly Working Environment with Clear Lines of Authority
- Increasing Public Awareness of Summer Sports Camp through Social Responsibility (local scholarship programs, free clinics, etc.)
- Developing a Sense of Community Within and Around the Summer Sports Camp

Camp Tip

Because of the nature and scale of long-term objectives, as well as the limited resources of most sports camps, no more than four or five long-term objectives should be attempted. How many short-term actions/goals could be created for each long-term objective? Simply stated, how ever many it takes to accomplish that particular long-term objective. It may take a few short-term actions to reach a long-term objective, or it could take literally dozens. Once again, it all depends on the long-term objective.

Section 3: SWOT Analysis (Strengths, Weaknesses, Opportunities, and Threats)

A SWOT analysis, which is an evaluation of a camp's internal strengths and weaknesses, and external opportunities and threats, is an essential part of establishing the future direction of the camp. "It relates to the firm's capabilities—or lack of them—and how they may be leveraged to create potential growth (opportunities) and factors that could negatively affect the firm (threats)."[8]

A major component of a feasibility study (discussed in Chapter 2) is the potential summer sports camp's SWOT analysis. The camp plan's SWOT analysis (whose foundation is in the feasibility study's SWOT) should answer the following questions:

- What are the attractive aspects of the company's situation?
- What aspects are of the most concern?
- Are the company's internal strengths and competitive assets sufficiently strong to enable it to compete successfully?
- Are the company's weaknesses and competitive deficiencies of small consequence and readily correctable, or could they prove fatal if not remedied soon?
- Do the company's strengths outweigh its weaknesses by an attractive margin?
- Does the company have attractive market opportunities that are well suited to its internal strengths? Does the company lack the competitive assets to pursue the most attractive opportunities?
- All things considered, where on a 1 to 10 (where 1 is alarmingly weak and 10 is exceptionally strong) do the company's overall situation and future prospects rank?[9]

Thanks to questions like these, a SWOT analysis will provide a durable basis for the camp, both now and in the future.

Section 4: Operating Systems

Table 4.4 lists the five components that make up the operating systems section of a summer sports camp plan.

Table 4.4: Summer Camp Operating Systems

Part 1: Human Resource Systems
Part 2: Marketing and Promotional Systems
Part 3: Financial Systems and Reports
Part 4: Sport Camp Management and Instruction Methods
Part 5: General Administration/Policies and Procedures

Part 1: Human Resource Systems

The human resource component of the camp plan is possibly the most far-reaching element of a quality operation and its sustained profitability. A camp administrator should consider the human resource element when assembling a team.

> In many cases, the business plan process will help you identify the gaps that exist on your team. It is rare for a founding entrepreneur to have all the competencies needed to launch a successful business. In fact, research suggests that ventures launched by teams are more likely to become sustainable businesses than those launched by individuals.[10]

With that said, the selection, improvement, and evaluation of your summer sports camp's human resource team is a critical responsibility.

© Stylephotographs | Dreamstime.com

The human resource segment is a plan within the camp's overall plan. The human resource planning process consists of four basic steps:

1. Determine the impact of the organization's objectives on specific organizational units.

2. Define skills, expertise, and total number of employees (demand for human resources) required to achieve the organizational and departmental objectives.

3. Determine the additional (net) human resource requirements in light of the organization's current human resources.

4. Develop an action plan to meet the anticipated human resource needs.[11]

A camp's human resource actions can consist of the following, without necessarily being limited to these elements:

- Equal Employment Opportunity compliance systems;
- new administration, staff, and clinician recruitment and selection systems;
- internal structure and promotional systems;
- human resource information processing systems (compliance);
- new camp employee orientation systems;
- state-of-the-art, sport-specific training systems;
- performance appraisal systems (for all internal stakeholders);
- compensation and negotiated contract systems (wage, benefit, etc.);
- uniform disciplinary systems; and
- camp safety and health systems.

Each human resource plan will selectively pick and choose human resource areas that will have the greatest impact on camp goals. (Human resource systems and management will be covered in detail in Chapters 8 and 9.)

Part 2: Marketing and Promotional Systems

The importance of the marketing component of the summer sports camp plan can be best described as follows:

> Entrepreneurs, especially inventors, often believe that their business concepts are so spectacular that promoting their product or service won't be necessary—sort of build-it-and-they-will-come attitude, especially if what you're building is the proverbial better mousetrap. . . . [P]otential investors, staff, and partners won't be convinced that your idea can succeed until you've established well-researched and effective methods of contacting your customer—and the assurance that once you've reached them, you can convince them to buy your product or service.[12]

While Chapters 10, 11, and 12 will be devoted to marketing concepts, it is important to examine them as components of the camp plan. The business subject of marketing is broken down into four factors, known as the *4 Ps of marketing* or the *marketing mix:*

- Product
- Price
- Place
- Promotion

The first of the 4 Ps, *product,* is typically the one element camp administrators devote their maximum effort in forming and improving. All subsequent marketing actions stem from it. The product is a quality camp program. Because we are flooded with promotional information, people (especially Americans) sometimes can be "duped" into buying products that are of low quality and value. Not so much with summer sports camps. In the most elementary language, if a camp is not good, the customers will stay away no matter what promotional tactics are utilized.

The second of the 4 Ps, *price,* is developed from the same logic. The more in demand the product, the higher the price the consumer will pay for the product. The greater the quality and demand for a camp, the more inclined the consumer will be to pay a higher price to attend it.

The third of the 4 Ps, *place,* is ordinarily controlled by several external factors. For example, if the summer sports camp is an institutional one, what league, conference, or geographic region one's athletic program is located will determine the facility (or facilities) used by the camp. Place (or *product distribution*) comes from the reality that the more visible and in demand a camp is, the less impact a location or facility has.

The final component of the marketing mix, *promotion,* is an element on which camp administrators can have the most influence, and it is the one area of the marketing mix that needs to be expressly spelled out in the camp plan. The key is to have the first three Ps in the marketing mix established. If one has a quality product at an acceptable price and locale, then it is up to the administrator's own resourcefulness, creativity, and effort to promote it. Is funding consequential in promotion? It is significant but not imperative. Any advertising executive will state that the ultimate goal of any promotional campaign is to secure and enlarge positive word of mouth about the product. Can a summer sports camp achieve this without major funding? Yes. Would it be easier to implement promotion with relevant funding? Undoubtedly. Yet, a camp administrator cannot let a lack of funding interfere with promotion.

© Icefields | Dreamstime.com

Marketing will be presented in more detail later, but for now consider what resources are going to be available for marketing and promotion in advance, and then formulate a strategy to squeeze every dollar available. For camps with minimal dollars, concepts such as employing current campers and their families, developing distinct logos, composing and distributing fliers, and verbally publicizing the camp are essential. Additionally, one can utilize low-cost promotional tactics:

1. Personal selling to persuade sports clubs and school teams to attend

2. Attending and participating in community functions

3. Making publicity speeches

4. Utilizing former program athletes and campers

5. Building a relationship with local media and developing a news release system

These are all cost-effective promotional techniques for summer sports camp. Once again, camp administrators and all personnel must be inventive and resourceful.

After a summer sports camp's marketing mix has been established, the marketing subdivision of a camp plan needs to be constructed. A camp administrator has two choices. The marketing section of a camp plan can do either of the following:

1. Incorporate the entire detailed marketing plan for the summer sports camp. These comprehensive documents break down the marketing mix:

   • Target marketing and demographics

   • Evaluation of competition

   • Customer profiles

   • Detailed elaboration of the marketing mix

2. Summarize the marketing plan. This approach keeps marketing and its planning as an independent document while providing a broad overview in the camp plan.

Part 3: Financial Systems and Reports

FINANCIAL PROJECTIONS.

Financial Planning is budgeting. There There are two explicit ways of budgeting:

Method 1: Calculate all of the 0camp's foreseeable expenditures, then total the amount; that result is the targeted income (break-even) amount.

Method 2: Estimate the camp's income (or total money available), then attempt to modify expenses within that amount.

The budgeting concept is that simple. The difficulty comes from how to hash out one's conclusions and how accurate one can be at predicting the summer sports camp's future. For a lucky few, they just know how to guesstimate, and their calculations are, by and large, accurate. The majority, however, needs to budget through concrete calculations.

While the budgeting concepts are covered throughout the book, here are some basic rules for developing a budget.

1. Base beginning projections in recorded facts. Usually, the amount spent or received in previous years is a good basis.

2. Always forecast high on projected expenses and low on projected income/revenue.

3. Get solid dollar amounts whenever possible. This might mean additional phone calls and leg work, but the effort will provide more accurate projections. Furthermore, whenever possible, get all quotes in writing.

4. Always anticipate miscellaneous expenses. The amount of miscellaneous or float dollars should be projected at 5–10% of the total amounts.

5. Anticipate all budget line items before computing dollar amounts. Attempt to incorporate every realistic expense and income source.

6. Triple-check all calculations.

7. Keep organized files for back-up and confirmation of budget amounts.

The camp plan should not only include budgets and projections, but also short narrative explanations of each item and how those estimates were obtained. While financial projections are future oriented, financial statements are historic records of what was actually received and expensed by the camp. The importance of including this type of information is in the validation of the current budget projections. Additionally, the numerical comparison between what happened during the camp and what was predicted to happen provides the administrators with an opportunity to explain variances.

The extent to which budgets are constructed depends greatly on the type and size of the summer sports camp as well as the level of expertise the camp administrator has in budgeting and financial statement accounting. The explanation of all of the different possible financial statements and numerical forecasting techniques moves beyond the scope of this book. However, a fundamental working knowledge of budgeting is critical for camp administration.

FINANCIAL OPERATING SYSTEMS.

Financial operating systems are used to compile financial information about a business and reporting this information to users. The six major steps of the accounting process are analyzing, recording, classifying, summarizing, reporting, and interpreting.

Analyzing is looking at events that have taken place and thinking about how they affect the business.

Recording is entering financial information about events into the accounting system. Although this can be done with paper and pencil, most businesses use computers to perform routine record-keeping operations.

Classifying is sorting and grouping similar items together rather than merely keeping a simple, diary-like record of numerous events.

Summarizing is bringing the various items of information together to determine results.

Reporting is telling the results. In accounting, it is common to use tables of numbers to report results.

Interpreting is deciding the meaning and importance of the information in various reports. This may include percentage analyses and the use of ratios to help explain how pieces of information relate to one another.[13]

While components of the financial operating systems will be discussed throughout the text, it is critical to identify what basic systems will be utilized—computerized, in most cases—and what factors will be prioritized in the camp plan.

Part 4: Sport Camp Management and Instruction Methods

The camp management and instruction methods section of the camp plan is as much philosophical as it is physical. Philosophically, a camp administrator must break down the overall management outlook and operational doctrine, using the vision, mission, and value statements. This section of the plan should discuss attitudes and behavioral expectations of all management personnel. Items such as daily planning, organizing and structuring activities, assigning personnel, leading staff and clinicians, and controlling all aspects of camp operation need to be elaborated in the plan. Additionally, the concept of team management needs to be examined.

While camp instruction will be discussed in Chapter 15, in the camp planning stage, a camp administrator must present the philosophical position the entire camp will take in terms of instruction methods. Bette Logsdon (as cited by Bonnie Pettifor on page 13 of her 1999 book, *Physical Education Methods for Classroom Teachers*) has six philosophical statements that can be applied to a summer camp's instruction methods.

1. The learner is an individual, and his or her individuality varies from day to day, task to task, and moment to moment.

2. As teachers, we must respect the integrity of the learner and accept responsibility for the education of this whole being.

3. We need to dedicate our talents, time, and energy to each child, permitting him or her to become an increasingly independent learner, and thereby helping him or her to achieve full potential.

4. The learner is capable of making decisions; therefore, we are responsible for helping the learner develop the ability to make reasoned choices so that he or she can adjust to his or her role appropriately as his or her social and physical surroundings change.

5. Each child may develop the understanding and skills essential to progression at different times through different experiences.

6. To be meaningful to the child, physical education teachers must provide experiences that improve his or her ability to move, that engage thought processes, and that contribute positively to both his or her developing value system and to the esteem with which he or she regards self and others.[14]

Part 5: General Administration/Policies and Procedures

While the camp plan's previous section—"Management and Instruction Method"—is philosophical, the General Administration/Policies and Procedure component of the plan is definitive. This section covers major and, depending on the detail required, minor policies and procedures (how-to's) for the camp.

The text *Crafting and Executing Strategy: The Quest for Competitive Advantage* highlights the importance of developing program policies and procedures by stating that well-conceived policies and operating procedures facilitate strategy execution in three ways:

1. They provide top-down guidance regarding how things need to be done.

2. They help ensure consistency in how execution-critical activities are performed.

3. They promote the creation of a work climate that facilitates good strategy execution.[15]

While policies and procedures are usually listed together in a summer sports camp plan, they are two separate elements. In straightforward terms, policies are more in line with camp rules that guide behavior (people oriented) while procedures are steps that explain how to perform camp functions (task oriented).

As a camp administrator, the most significant aspect for the development and the use of policies would be dealing with other staff, administrators, coaches, clinicians, camp athletes, and outside consultants. For example, the different areas in policy design and execution concerning clinicians would contain all types of behavioral expectations. From items such as expected arrival and departure times, session preparation, camper and parent interactions, administrative responsibilities, and camp representation in the community, policies need to be developed and continuously stressed.

The concentration and range of policy items within a camp plan are determined by the operation's philosophies, position, operational environment, history, and traditions. Some areas may be highlighted more than others. For example, the policies section of the camp plan could clarify specific policies on clinician-parental communication as well as a detailed disciplinary system for violations that includes verbal warnings, written warnings, suspension, and expulsion. In such an environment, each clinician should have an absolute understanding of the consequences and possible conflicts of parental interactions. The camp's policies should be in well-structured, plain language to avoid any misinterpretations.

Procedures are step-by-step actions taken to perform specific tasks. Camp administrators should strive to have straightforward procedures in areas of administrative

> **Camp Tip**
>
> Policy and procedure manuals are only beneficial if they are acknowledged, established, and applied. Constantly re-emphasize the camp's commitment to its policies and procedures.

functions, session training, equipment use, facility utilization (set-up and breakdown), incident reporting, etc. The biggest dividend in sound procedures for camp functions is uniformity. Uniformity saves time, coordinates activities, and minimizes frustration and stress that arise from disorganization.

© Flimfoto | Dreamstime.com

APPENDIX 4.1: OTHER ELEMENTS OF A SUMMER SPORTS CAMP PLAN

Title Page

The title page/cover of the camp plan is an informative ingredient, as well as a relevant presentation component. Features can include the following:

- Camp name (school, university, club name affiliation)
- Operational address, phone, email addresses
- Date of plan
- Camp logo
- Primary camp entrepreneurs/ administrators
- Copy numbers (which are essential for tracking camp plans)

Table of Contents

Because of the size of camp plans, a table of contents is indispensable. Headings with corresponding page numbers provide readers with an easy way to access specific information without going through the entire document.

Key Players/Organizational Chart

The camp plan segment titled Key Players/Organizational Chart has two independent but closely interconnected elements. The subsection of key players is a conventional job description behind each administration, clinician, and staff position in the organization (e.g., camp director, head clinician, coach, newsletter publisher, public relations director, etc.). The second subsection is a standard organizational chart. The diagram should display the structure of the camp, who is accountable to whom, and who is answerable for each division below (chain of command). When combined, these elements furnish everyone with clearly defined roles, positions, and camp structure.

ENDNOTES

1. Scarborough, N. M. (2011). *Essentials of entrepreneurship and small business management* (6th edition), p. 74. Upper Saddle River, NJ: Prentice Hall.

2. King, J. B. (2000). *Business plans to game plans: A practical system for turning strategies into action* (2nd edition), p. 40. Los Angeles, CA: Silver Lake Publishing.

3. Bateman, T. S., & Snell, S. A. (2011). *Management: Leading and collaborating in a competitive world* (9th edition), p. 136. New York, NY: McGraw-Hill/Irwin.

4. Fogg, C. D. (1999). *Implementing your strategic plan: How to turn "intent" into effective action for sustainable change*, p. 234. New York, NY: AMACOM.

5. Kinicki, A., & Williams, B. K. (2003). *Management: A practical introduction*, p. 153. New York, NY: McGraw-Hill/Irwin.

6. Rue, L. W., & Byars, L. L. (2009). *Management: Skills and applications* (13th edition), p. 135. New York, NY: McGraw-Hill/Irwin.

7. Yow, D. A., Migliore, R. H., Bowden, W. W., Stevens, R. E., & Loudin, D. L. (2000). *Strategic planning for college athletics*, pp. 52-53. Binghamton, NY: Haworth Press.

8. Allen, K. R. (2007). *Growing and managing a small business: An entrepreneurial perspective*, p. 64. Boston, MA: Houghton Mifflin.

9. Thompson, A. A., Peteraf, M. A., Gamble, J. E., & Strickland, A. J. (2014). *Crafting and executing strategy: The quest of competitive advantage* (19th edition), p. 96. New York, NY: McGraw Hill/Irwin.

10. Timmons, J. A., Zacharakis, A., & Spinelli, S. (2004). *Business plans that work: A guide for small business*, p. 103. New York, NY: McGraw-Hill/Irwin.

11. Byars, L. L., & Rue, L. W. (2008). *Human resource management* (9th edition), p. 90. New York, NY: McGraw-Hill/Irwin.

12. Rogoff, E. G. (2004). *Bankable business plans*, p. 43. New York, NY: Thompson/Texere.

13. Heintz, J. A., & Parry, R. W. (2002). *College accounting* (2nd edition), p 3. Cincinnati, OH: South-Western.

14. Logsdon, B. (1997). Physical education unit plans for preschool-kindergarten. In Pettifor, B. (1999). *Physical education methods for classroom teachers*, p. 13. Champaign, IL: Human Kinetics.

15. Thompson, A. A., Peteraf, M. A., Gamble, J. E., & Strickland, A. J. (2014). *Crafting and executing strategy: The quest of competitive advantage* (19th edition), pp. 319-320. New York, NY: McGraw Hill/Irwin.

ADMINISTRATION SYSTEMS

For a camp to work properly, sound administration systems need to be constructed and employed. Camp systems such as registration, filing, and accounting are essential and universal to all camps. Whether by hard copy or computerization, these areas need to have a logical flow to guide camp employees and clearly report all summer sports camp activities. Their accuracy can have a significant impact for the current and future operation.

CHAPTER

5

Administration Systems and Registration

INTRODUCTION TO SYSTEMS

Systems are necessary elements for all businesses, sports camps included. Systems can best be described as

> the blueprint of a building or house, it consists of all the specifications that give the business its form and structure. . . . [S]ystems may have many possible designs. Each design represents a unique blend of technical and organizational components. What makes one design superior to others is the ease and efficiency with which it fulfills user requirements within a specific set of technical, organizational, financial, and time constraints.[1]

© Alphaspirit | Dreamstime.com

In other words, systems are the real processes the camp uses to function. Without the most basic systems, it is virtually impossible to operate a camp. Strong systems:

- provide a camp its structure, from big-picture objectives to small-picture actions;

- have an overwhelming impact on a camp's productivity and working efficiency;

- contribute to the professionalism of the operation for both internal and external participants; and

- have a tremendous impact on the camper's experience.

In the textbook *Successful Project Management,* Jack Gido and James Clements describe the six-step system development lifecycle. While these six steps can be enormously complex in a large corporation or conglomerate, they can be easily adapted to the business of a camp. The six steps in the system development lifecycle are summarized as follows:

1. *Problem definition.* Data are gathered and analyzed, and problems and opportunities are clearly defined.

2. *System analysis.* The development team defines the scope of the system to be developed, interviews potential users, studies the existing system (which might be manual), and defines the user requirements.

3. *System design.* Several alternative conceptual designs are produced that describe input, processing, output, hardware, software, and database at a high level.

4. *System development.* The actual system is brought into existence.

5. *System testing.* After individual modules within the system have been developed, testing can begin. . . . Once the users and the developers are convinced that the system is error-free, the system can be implemented.

6. *System implementation.* The existing system is replaced with the new, improved system, and users are trained.[2]

The system design lifecycle is a commonsense foundation for a camp administrator to follow when constructing the systems that will be the basis of the camp's operation. The importance of the system being designed will influence the amount of depth, work, and time allotted to the six steps. Understandably, minor camp systems will have less time and effort given to them than major camp systems. However, if the six steps in the system-designed lifecycle are followed, minor camp systems will also have a solid foundation and functionality.

General System Design Guidelines

Prior to developing individual systems for camp operation, some general guidelines must be reviewed that are universal to all camp operations.

Guideline 1: As a rule, all systems should be developed and ready to apply (step 6 of the system design lifecycle) prior to accepting registrations or any other camp function. For example, beginning to take enrollments without a sustainable registration system in place could be disastrous. Registration information could be unaccounted for, payments misclassified, critical camp documentation misplaced (or worse, omitted), camp athletes placed in incorrect skill groups, etc. Any one of these issues could have serious liability and public relations problems for the current and future camp enterprise.

Guideline 2: The more complete the system, the less chance for wasted opportunities. One of the worst circumstances that could happen to a camp is to have a strong demand for its services but not have the systems in place to handle that demand. When camp systems are being designed, they should be created with the camp's maximum capacity in mind. Even though the camp might not reach that capacity, a camp administrator will know that he or she is not missing any opportunities or having to make any mid-course corrections to support growth.

Guideline 3: In addition to the systems that are universal to all camps, each individual camp will have its own specific systems. The factors that determine which particular and distinct systems a camp can have encompass

- the particular sport's activities and constraints,
- entrepreneurial verses institutional system requirements,
- day versus overnight camps,
- governing body of the sport's requirements, and
- miscellaneous factors unique to the camp's individual environment.

Guideline 4: Because a majority of systems deal with information, a camp's system design must be *unconditionally committed to data security.* The two major camp areas that are crucial to maintain data security are business information on the camp's operations and personal information on personnel such as administrators, staff, clinicians, and external participants such as parents and campers. No matter what type of system is adopted—hardcopy, computerized, or a combination of both—system safeguards such as restricted access security levels, cryptographic or hidden file coding, strict retrieval protocol, locked hardcopy information, and secure long-term storage are just a few of the data security considerations. The problem in data security is balancing data retrieval simplicity with the security concerns.

Guideline 5: As previously stated, camp systems should always have the end-user in mind. They should be as stress free, orderly, organized, easy to understand, and 100% targeted as possible. With this in mind, it is advisable to have the people who will be working the systems involved in the systems design process.

Guideline 6: In the construction of systems, avoid the notion that systems either need to be 100% paper or 100% computerized. Camp systems should be developed with the camp's mission in mind and the most appropriate functionality for that particular camp. Most camps work best with a blend of computerization and hardcopy records.

Camp Tip

It is a sensible tactic in the camp's development stage to define all of the required systems, both universal and camp-specific. By having a definite list, a camp administrator can visualize the systems that need to be in place and assign construction to the appropriate personnel.

Each method has its value and should complement the other. For example, if a camp's systems are primarily hardcopy, one should strongly consider having computerized scanning capabilities and cloud storage back-up. Conversely, if a camp's systems are predominantly computerized or web based, a hardcopy back-up system of vital spreadsheets, forms, and miscellaneous information would be worthwhile to maintain.

Guideline 7: For a camp's smooth performance, administration systems should have unity, flow, and compatibility. While each system focuses on a critical camp area, it needs to have a balanced relationship with all other systems. Think of it this way: A camp is an assembly of systems. It only takes one of these systems to be out of sync with the rest to slow, damage, or shut down a camp. Additionally, any system that does not add relevant value to the camp or the camper's experience should be considered a waste of valuable resources.

With these general guidelines outlined, the remaining component of this section will cover major systems that are common to all summer sports camp operations:

- Camp registration sSystems
- General concepts for filing systems
- Budgets, recordkeeping, and accounting systems

Special Note: Chapters 8 and 9 will be dedicated to the development of human resource systems, and Chapters 10, 11, 12 will be devoted to marketing systems.

OVERVIEW OF CAMP REGISTRATION SYSTEMS

Having a well thought-out, ordered registration system is required for a discussion of precamp administrative functions. The registration system should be considered more than just paperwork and forms. Behind the forms, documents, and files are children. That is why it is critical to have a registration system that is as client friendly as possible while being thorough in its detail. It needs to have a logical progression that leads the parent and camper step by step through the entire registration process and policies (see Table 6.1 for detailed list). Additionally, a sound registration system keeps parents and campers informed through targeted, individualized communication about procedures, current status, and outstanding items, all while maintaining the system's reliability and documentation.

Hardcopy Paper and Computerized Registration Tools

The three principal camp registration tool categories are (1) traditional paper based, (2) integrated/combined software packages and online systems, and (3) originally constructed, web-based instruments.

Traditional Paper-Based Registration Tools

In the age of computers, smart phones, and tablets, can paper-based registration tools still be relevant for a summer sports camp? They can and often are enormously applicable for a summer sports camp. For small or new camps with limited resources, traditional paper registration tools can be very appropriate. Hardcopy tools and paper-based instruments could consist of

- hanging file folders and filing cabinets;
- pre-printed forms and documents;
- postage delivery;
- hand-tabulated confirmations;
- camper information spreadsheets;
- scripted accounting forms, ledgers, and records;
- letters and post card reminders;
- and so on.

The key to the efficient use of paper-based tools is in their preparation and organization. For example, say a camp is at the stage where registration forms are coming in. Instead of building individualized packets for each parent/camper as they are accepted, a camp should have prepackaged camp envelopes with all relevant forms, payment information, registration procedures, and deadlines spelled out in detail. After the administrator records all registration and payment information for that individual camper and inserts a basic confirmation sheet, the packet is then addressed, stamped, and mailed. To simplify the return of documents to the operation, provide a self-addressed stamped envelope in the packet for campers to use.

The disadvantages of paper registration tools are obvious. They can be unwieldy if a camp operation is large. A disorganized camp venture can have substantially more openings for human error. Subsequently, correcting human errors can be extremely time consuming and could leave the customers with a negative feeling about the camp. For example, if the administrator forgets to include an essential form in the registration packets (e.g., the camp medical form) the administrator will then have to send, by hand, medical forms to each and every registered camper, as well as correct all of the prepackaged registration envelopes. This can be time consuming and potentially expensive. Other disadvantages of paper registration tools could relate to their perishability, keeping an ample supply of forms without having an excess of wasted supplies, storage and space requirements, and speed and versatility in generating reports.

Integrated Software Packages and Online Systems

Prebundled registration and camp management software can add a powerful ingredient to a summer sports camp's efficiency and productivity. The companies that offer camp registration and management software furnish a wide selection of packages and, in some cases, these packages can be tailored to one's operation. The depth and application of software bundles varies from company to company. Some are strictly for registration and billing, while others furnish computerized systems for all areas of a summer sports camp's operation. All-inclusive camp administration software could include software that deals with registration, scheduling, billing, medical processes,

As previously discussed, even the most computerized systems should utilize paper back-ups, especially for emergency forms that might need to be retrieved at a moment's notice.

© Maziama | Dreamstime.com

marketing, communication, or other areas. Understandably, the more software and online system components provided, the higher the price tag.

The number of possible suppliers of summer sports camp software is considerable. There are two types of registration and camp management software businesses. The first sells camp registration and management software outright to camps. Often these companies make available some modifications to their product but most are generic packages for commonplace use, similar to purchasing any type of prepackaged computer software. In general, these packages are more than sufficient for most camp operations. The second software business provides registration and camp management online through its web site and server. Typically, for a monthly fee, a camp administrator sets up and operates camp registration and any other system within the company's site. The primary advantage of online registration and camp management is having the summer sports camp's systems available from any remote point at any time.

There are some significant issues when selecting a software or online provider:

- **Cost:** This can be, and frequently is, a central factor in the type of software selected and what components it has.

- **Learning Curve:** How long it will take to get up and running on a specific registration and camp management software system is a noteworthy consideration.

- **Hardware Requirements:** For all software, there is hardware. A concern for the selection of a software package is the current operation's hardware capabilities, as well as its compatibility with a particular software package.

- **Software Support:** The nature and level of support provided by a software vendor is a serious consideration when purchasing a system or package.

- **Bells and Whistles:** A camp administrator should avoid being caught up in the sales pitch for additional bells and whistles attached to software systems.

- **Long-Term Objectives:** Software should be based on current needs and future goals of the camp. Prior to purchasing a software system, a general review of the summer sports camp plan would be wise.

Appendix 5.1 has a broad list of companies that offer different generic and sports-specific registration and camp management software and online systems.

Individualized Web-Based Tools

A camp may determine that it wants to create its own Internet-based registration and camp management web page. This ground-up tactic has one overriding advantage: control. Simply stated, the web page is totally under the influence and management of the camp administrators and staff. Camp components can be added and deleted internally at a moment's notice. Designs and promotional materials can be customized and updated as the camp evolves. Communication with current and potential campers can be done instantaneously within the system's database. In other words, what the web page will be used for is entirely up to the camp's personnel.

Web page functionality can range from minimal to comprehensive. Individualized summer sports camp web pages can include

- all custom-made forms such as registration, medical, emergency, and so on to and from parents and campers;
- marketing and promotional materials, such as camp brochures and videos;
- the primary communication system for camp administration and staff, parents, and campers;
- program information and schedules;
- payment options;
- maps and location specifics (parking, registration areas, athletic facilities, dorms, etc.); and
- staff and clinician bios.

The key to a successful and well-designed web page is planning. Knowing what the camp envisions for the web page, laying down the criteria for its use, and then providing that information in a detailed format is the formula for its development. For internal creation and management of the site, it is ideal if the summer sports camp can have someone with web design experience on staff. If not, the page will need to be constructed by a third party.

APPENDIX 5.1: INTEGRATED SOFTWARE PACKAGES AND ONLINE MANAGEMENT SITES

The following are examples of companies that offer camp registration software and online camp management services, both for sports and general summer camps. Whether they are for athletic or recreational camps, each product line can be adapted to one's particular operation.

Camp Tip

When putting together a camp's final registration system, if resources allow, blended use of all three media—paper, software, and web based—could be the best method. The fundamental principle in blending registration tools should center on what is best for the customer (i.e., parents and campers).

Special Note: Numerous software and web-based packages offer complete camp administration systems that include, but are not limited to, registration, scheduling, billing, medical processes, and communication.

ABC Sports Camp: Online Event Management

www.abcregistrations.com

Active Network Camps

www.activecamps.com

Camp Brain

www.campbrain.com

Camp Site: Camp Management Software

www.campmanagement.com

CampSOFT Camp Management

www.getphysicalsoftware.com

EZ – Camp @

www.ezcamp2.com

My Online Camp

www.myonlinecamp.com

On-Q Software

www.on-qsoftware.com

Proclass

www.proclassonline.com

SDI Camps

www.sdicamps.com

ENDNOTES

1. Loundon, K. C., & Laudon, J. P. (2010). *Management information systems: Managing the digital firm* (11th edition), p. 491. Upper Saddle River, NJ: Pearson/ Prentice Hall.
2. Gido, J., & Clements, J. P. (1999). *Successful project management,* pp. 205-206. Cincinnati, OH: South-western. p. 205-206

Registration Systems

REGISTRATION PROCESS

Table 6.1 is a stage-by-stage registration process that can be adopted by any camp.

Stage 1: Receiving and Accepting Registrations

Registration Forms

Figure 6.1 details the components of a camp registration form. As noted, delivery of registration forms can be through traditional methods (mail, brochures, handouts, etc.) or through electronic distribution (emails, web pages, integrated software systems, etc.).

Establishing Deposit and Refund Policies

A camp deposit, centered on a time schedule, should be included to hold a spot for participating camp athletes. A payment timetable could entail the following dates:

- 6 months (or registration sign-up) to 3 months prior to camp—50% deposit required
- 3 months to 1 month prior to camp—75% deposit required
- 1 month to camp date—100% paid in full

A deposit schedule should also come with a complete refund policy. A workable refund policy on deposits and payments could parallel the above timetable by the following criteria:

Table 6.1. **General Registration Process for Summer Sports Camps**

Stage 1: Receiving and Accepting Registrations

- Registration Forms
- Establishing Deposit and Refund Policies
- Initial Camper Designation and Group Placement
- Record Payment and Calculate Balances (Accounts Receivable Policies)
- Initial Folders for Campers

Stage 2: Participant Documentation

- Confirmation Sheets
- Medical Questionnaire
- Medical Release Form
- Camp Insurance Documentation
- Code of Conduct
- All Other Camp-Specific Documentation

Stage 3: Registration Communication

- Email, Phone, Post Card Practices
- Reminders:
  - Camp Attendance
  - Dates and Locations
  - Items Due
  - Important Camp Items to Bring
  - Updates and Changes
  - Miscellaneous Information

Stage 4: Event-Day Registration

- Known and Centrally Located Registration and Check-In Area
- Staffing Requirements
- Complete Inventory of Supplies and Blank Registration Forms
- Distribution Area for Camp Items and Promotional Giveaways
- Computer and Hardcopy Systems Available to Check In Athletes and Confirm Registration Documentation
- Facilitation of Traffic Flow from Registration Area to Sports-Specific Instructional Areas
- Final Group Rosters to Head Clinician and Group Leaders

- 6 months to 3 months prior to camp: 100% refund available
- 3 months to 1 month prior to camp: 75% refund available
- 1 month to 2 weeks prior to camp: 50% refund available
- 2 weeks to camp date: 0% refund

Because camps often have limited space, camper cancellations from two weeks to the camp's start date should lose all deposits because fixed and most variable costs cannot be recaptured from that point forward.

Initial Camper Designation and Group Placement

Once registrations are received, placement of athletes into identifiable camp sessions and rosters should be completed. Each camp session should have its own participant spreadsheet with its maximum overall size and clinician-to-camper ratio outlined in advance of registration. Once camp sessions are filled, an immediate contact with the parents or guardians should be made to either rechannel participants into other sessions or cancel the registrations and send back deposits/payments.

Section 1: Camper/Participant Information

- Complete Name (first, middle, last)
- Address (street, city, state, zip)
- Phone Numbers (home and cell)
- Emails
- Gender
- Birth Date
- Grade and School Name
- Apparel Size (if applicable)
- Physical Attributes (sport specific)
  - Height
  - Weight
  - Vertical Leap
  - Bench
  - 40-Yard Time
- Medical Issues (to be asked in detail in Stage 2 forms)
- Level of Participant's Skills (generic [beginner, intermediate, advanced] or sport-specific classifications)

Section 2: Parental/Guardian Information

- Complete Names (first, middle, last)
- Address (street, city, state, zip)
- Phone Numbers (home, work, cell)
- Emails (all possible)

Section 3: Emergency Contact Persons (2) (besides parents/guardians)

- Names and Phone Numbers

Section 4: Camp Information *(check-box or circle format)*

- Name of Camp(s)
- Date(s)
- Session Time(s)
- Food Program (if applicable)
- Accommodations (for overnight camps)
- Cost and Total Due

Section 5: Payment Information

- Deposit Policy
- Payment Method
  - Checks/Money Orders (made out to...)
  - Credit Card
  - Name on Card
  - Type of Card
  - Card Number
  - Expiration Date
  - Signature
- Refund Policy

Section 6: Participant Agreement

- Narrative Summer Sports Camp Agreement Statement
- Parental/Guardian Signature
- Date

Section 7: Return Camp Address

- Administration's/Registrar's Name (attention to:)
- Address
- Phone Number
- Email/Web (if applicable)

Figure 6.1. **Components of a Summer Sports Camp Registration Form**

Record Payment/Calculate Balances

The next step in the initial registration stage should be to record and calculate all payments and balances remaining on the account. The camp administrator should establish an accounts receivable folio for each participant, either through a computerized accounting software package or through a manual ledger system.

Initial Folders for Campers

Finally, the administrator should generate a computerized and/or hardcopy folder for each camper participating in the camp. The file will be the primary reference for all financial documentation and camp-specific information.

Camp Tip

For security, constantly gather and lock up all payments made to the camp. Payment and check safeguards should be organized and secured. Periodic bank deposits should be supervised by at least two camp staff members. All camp deposits should have bank confirmations.

© Winterling | Dreamstime.com

Stage 2: Participant Documentation

Confirmation Sheets

While they might seem unneeded, camp confirmation forms verify registration information and supply parents and campers with a game plan for documentation, payments, and processes. Specifically, they supply parents and campers with

- confirmation of the camp sessions purchased. This restatement can avoid any possible confusion and uncomfortable misunderstandings.

- balances due and payment schedules. By providing this information, parents can budget and plan out payment disbursements.

- check-in procedures, times, locations, and drop-off protocol. This knowledge can lessen parents' and campers' anxiety the beginning of camp.

- documents due. Providing information of all of the summer sports camp documents due can greatly enhance efficiency in this critical camp area.

- items to bring—and to avoid bringing. Providing a list of sport-specific items can minimize fear and maximize the camper's experience.

Medical Questionnaire/Medical Release Forms

MEDICAL QUESTIONNAIRES

If the camp is associated with an academic institution, the institution will likely possess a standardized medical questionnaire. It is strongly suggested that the institution's medical questionnaire be evaluated and signed off on by the camp's medical and athletic training personnel. Simply stated, the camp's medical and training staff need to feel comfortable with the information specified on the medical questionnaire as it relates to youth athletes, the particular camp sport, and activities planned. If they do not feel satisfied, they should have an unobstructed ability to modify, alter, or amend the form. Obviously, any revisions should be discussed directly with the institution's athletic administration.

If the camp is a new entrepreneurial venture, it will need to construct a complete medical questionnaire form. The process should be twofold. The first step should have the camp administrator reviewing other medical questionnaires. Be warned that the volume of medical questionnaires for sport and recreational camps online is massive. From benchmarking similar sports camp questionnaires, one should construct a first draft questionnaire for the operation. The second step is the same as an institutional camp. Have the summer sports camp's medical and training staff critically assess the entire form, line by line.

MEDICAL RELEASE FORMS

Medical release forms (also known as *medical waivers* or *consent forms*) are legal documents that are essential to a summer sports camp. While the medical questionnaire provides camper-specific medical information, the medical release form is considered more of an authorization or permission document. Table 6.2 details some of

Camp Tip

The most important aspect of a medical questionnaire is its completeness. The questionnaire should cover all anticipated medical conditions and contingencies. In case of emergency, external medical personnel will be able to immediately review the document and be furnished with as much critical information as possible. Remember: Child safety is paramount for camp operation.

the possible components of a medical release form. It should be noted that since this is a legal document, it is vital that legal counsel examine and approve the final information and form.

Camp Insurance Documentation

While insurance will be covered in Chapter 13, it should be noted that all insurance documents and payments required for a camper's participation should be distributed in this stage of the registration process. The forms and additional cost required for camp coverage will be determined by the camp's insurance carrier.

Code of Conduct

In a perfect world, a code of conduct for the camp would not be necessary. Unfortunately, we do not live in a perfect world. Parents and campers must understand the camp's policies, behavioral guidelines, and consequences of certain actions and attitudes. It should be noted in the last sentence that the parents as well as the campers should be bound by a certain level of civility and decorum. With that said, Table 6.3 has a general subject template for a summer sports camp's Code of Conduct. It is up to the administrator, and the camp's history, which elements need to be emphasized.

Camp Tip

Under no conditions or circumstances should a camp allow an athlete to participate in any activities without a complete file with all the camp documentation. The liability exposure and implications to the operation, as well as to camp administration and staff, could be catastrophic. All returned medical forms should be reviewed by the camp's medical staff and certified athletic trainers prior to the beginning of any and all camp sessions. Medical staff concerns should be discussed immediately with all administrators, clinicians, and staff.

Table 6.2. **Categories of Information on a Medical Release Form**

- Camper Information
  - Name
  - Age/D.O.B.
  - Height/Weight/Physicality Information

- Emergency Contact Information
  - Parent's Name and Contact Information
  - Secondary Emergency Contact Information

- Camper's Physician/Pediatrician Information
  - Name
  - Address
  - Office Contact Information
  - After Hours/Emergency Contact Information

- Health Insurance Provider
  - Group Policy Number
  - ID Number

- Camper's Specific Conditions
  - Allergies, Immunization, Medications, Pre-existing Conditions

- Disclosure Statement for Release of Health Information
  - Parental Signature

- Emergency Medical Authorization Statement
  - Parental Signatures

- Notary Public Signature and Seal

Table 6.3. Foundations of a Summer Sports Camp Code of Conduct

- Citizenship and Respect for All Campers, Staff, and Instructors
- Positive Attitude and 100% Participation
- Respect for Property and Equipment
- Attendance and Tardy Policies
- Following Directions
- Wearing Sport Appropriate Athletic Apparel (as well as nonoffensive language on all clothing)
- Curfew and Housing Rules (if applicable)
- Unauthorized Leaving of Camp
- Rules on Electronics (cell phones, video games, mp3/iPods)
- Cleanliness (personal and public)
- Zero Tolerance Policy
  - Bullying
  - Drugs
  - Tobacco
  - Violence
  - Profanity
  - Sexual Harassment
  - Weapons
  - Ethnic or Racial Slurs
- Complying with All Federal, State, and Local Laws and Regulations
- Ramification Statement for Code of Conduct Violations
- Signatures of Parents and Campers (and dates)

Stage 3: Registration Communication

A crucial aspect of a camp is its proficiency in communicating with its registered customers, both parents and campers. Whether it is through email, phone, post cards, or letters, camp administrators need to establish and maintain open lines of communication. Information that needs to be imparted to parents and campers prior to the beginning of camp sessions can encompass the following:

- **Camp Attendance:** It is advisable to send out final reminders on camp sessions, dates, and times, approximately two weeks before camp is to start. These courtesy reminders show professionalism as well as clearing up any possible scheduling oversights and miscommunications.

- **Locations:** Camp directions, drop-off and pick-up points and procedures, and parking facilities should be sent out one week prior to a camp's commencement. These communication reminders can have substantial benefits come the first day of camp.

- **Items Due:** During the precamp stage, periodic exchanges of documents and forms with parents and campers is a practical administration tactic. These communications can stress the magnitude of completing these particular camp elements.

- **Important Camp Items to Bring:** If necessary, these reminder communications are helpful for parents to plan purchases of apparel and equipment for the camp.

- **Updates and Changes:** This is an essential communication function. All camp changes and updates need to be communicated immediately to affected parents and campers. It is advisable to get confirmation of these communications to avoid someone missing critical information.

© Devonyu | Dreamstime.com

Camp Tip

While other areas of camp systems can utilize other devices, it is recommended that the precamp communication method be through electronic channels. It is by far the best and simplest way to stay in contact with the entire camper/parent population. Messages can be sent at a moment's notice and targeted on specific camp topics. Additionally, responses can be instantaneous and tracked.

CHAPTER 6

- **Miscellaneous Information:** This area can encompass everything from staff and clinician adjustments to weather forecasts to public relations messages.

One warning on precamp communication: A camp administrator should avoid drowning parents and campers with excessive correspondence. It can be annoying, and important information could be disregarded along with "fluff" communications. Additionally, to avoid unwanted or redundant communications from numerous camp sources, a camp should have a communications director who handles all correspondence with parents and campers.

Stage 4: Event-Day Registration

Registration on the first day of camp should address the following issues and concerns:

1. *Have a centrally located and well-publicized registration area.* The camp's registration area and tables should be easily accessed by all parents and campers. If necessary, signage that directs parents and campers to the proper registration area and specific check-in tables should be positioned tactically throughout the facility and site. Furthermore, to avoid a chaotic atmosphere at the beginning of camp, the registration location should be spacious to facilitate peak arrival times.

2. *Staff the registration area with fully competent personnel.* It cannot be stated strongly enough: The people who are working the registration tables have to be absolutely proficient at the registration system. They should know all of the camp's documentation requirements, accounts receivable structure, group assignments, computer operations, filing systems, etc. It would only take one unqualified individual to cause a sizeable and extremely frustrating bottleneck of parents and campers. In large camps, it is worthwhile to have the camp's head registrar not work the registration tables but supervise the effective functioning of the system. Any questions and issues can be immediately handled and confusion can be avoided.

3. *Have a complete inventory of supplies and blank forms.* Another registration-day tactic to avoid parent-camper bottlenecks is to ensure that each registration table has an ample surplus of blank forms, files, and general supplies. Furthermore, it is advisable to have quick access to a high-capacity, multifunctional copier just in case of unanticipated registration volume.

4. *Set up a distribution area for camp items and promotional giveaways.* For smaller camps, this area could be staffed by one person (who could also work some other registration functions) and placed next to the registration area. For large camps with hundreds of campers and extensive promotional giveaways (t-shirts, bags, balls, towels,

Camp Tip

A standard rule for the final stage of a summer sports camp registration process must be that all campers go through a check-in process, even if their files and payments are complete. Once registration is complete, final reviewed rosters should be copied to all clinicians and instructors.

etc.), a separate location that is able to handle the promotional items inventory will need to be set up. This area will have its own dedicated staff. The process for merchandise distribution could be as follows:

a. Parent/Camper completes all registration criteria and checks in.

b. Once cleared, the registrar will give the parent/camper a color-coded merchandise voucher. The voucher will indicate the camper's name and what promotional items and sizes he or she will receive.

c. The parent/camper presents the voucher to the staff at the distribution area and receives his or her items. One option for large summer sports camps is to have each camper's items prepackaged in a promotional camp bag.

d. The vouchers are collected and counted by the staff to reconcile beginning and ending merchandise inventory.

5. *Keep registration areas mobile.* Registration-day equipment needs to be portable as well as completely functional. Registration equipment such as laptops and back-ups, file boxes, wheeled cabinets, and general supplies should be able to move in an instant. Mobility should not only be for set-up and breakdown, but for unforeseen registration possibilities such as inclement weather and facility changes.

6. *Facilitate traffic flow from registration area to sports-specific instructional areas.* Campers should seamlessly transition from camp registration locations to designated instructional areas (or to accommodations, if applicable). Signage, facility maps, and human guides can all be used to facilitate flow.

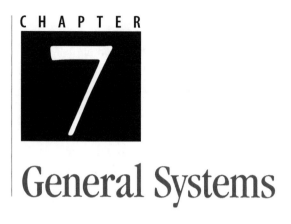

CHAPTER

7

General Systems

GENERAL CONCEPTS FOR FILING SYSTEMS

As discussed throughout this section, because of the escalating popularity of personal computers, filing now has developed into a matter of which flash drive, hard drive, or cloud system should be used to file information. However, even with access to the most reliable computer systems, sports camps should utilize a hardcopy filing system, typically a printout or other paper document of critical data. These materials must be catalogued in such a way that they can be located instantly with little or no effort by all administrators and staff members. The cardinal rule of filing is the simpler the better. Precision and orderliness in a filing system is critical: A disorderly and jumbled filing system can be worse than no filing system at all.

Costs associated with filing systems can be minimal. If ordered correctly, a five-drawer cabinet with basic hanging file folders can be more than enough to meet a camp's filing needs. To install a filing system, one needs to identify vital camp categories first and work toward smaller details within each classification. Hopefully, the camp will not have more than five or six vital classifications. For example, in most camp programs, some of the major categories would be camper's files, employee's files, accounting files, recordkeeping files, and general administration files.

While all files are critical to maintain, the most important files are the camper files. Campers' files can be subsectioned into camp groups (age, level, sessions, etc.) or filed all together in smaller operations. Whether subsectioned or not, these files should be in alphabetical order and as exhaustive as possible. Standardization of basic information for each file and camper is essential. The best way to accomplish standardization is through a file check-off list that has all of the important information listed. As items come in, the registrar checks that they have been received. Prior to the camp, a final file review should be done to confirm file completion. After the data has been uniformly filed, supplement each file with other subsequent individualized camper information.

Once the system has been refined, it is essential that all files are, from time to time, cleaned out. Files have a tendency to get cluttered with obsolete materials. Appropriate maintenance means going through each one and thinning out nonimportant information. Additionally, at the end of the camp, pull out yearly files and store them for future reference. Even though it is up to one's personal preference, it is advisable to retain archived files for at least three years. Availability of stored files should be in reverse chronological order, with the most recent years the easiest to retrieve.

To conclude this section, the 2001 article titled "Filing. . . like the beat. . . goes on. . . and on" has a list of pointers on managing paper and filing. The following is a summary of its concepts:

- Have a simple but complete filing system, one that makes sense to you.
- Always alphabetize. No matter what the structure of your filing system is, alphabetize within in it. It will save you time.
- Always color code for easy, quick identification. . . . Apply color coding even for a few files. As the number of files grows, the color system will make it easier to determine where a new file will go.
- Duplicating a document for filing in two different places creates more work, more bulk, and is seldom useful. Resist.
- Place most recent documents in the front of the file folder. . . . [T]he oldest documents will be in the back when it is time to purge files.
- Sometimes deciding where to file a document is tricky. Always ask yourself, "Where would I look for this if I need it?" Never ask, "Where should I put this?"
- File each document as you finish with it or file at the end of the day. Don't let filing pile up.
- Staple together documents on the same subject with the most current information on top. Don't use paperclips. . . . [T]hey can come off or catch on other papers in a file.
- Mark a discard date if you know when a document will become obsolete. Later you will know that you can throw it away without having to take time to read it.[1]

Additionally, to keep track of the categories of items filed and to be filed, post a single sheet of paper alongside the file cabinet with the categories and their breakdown. The filing breakdown could be in a simplified outline form. In addition to being a reference, the sorting document could act as a method of labeling

CHAPTER 7

file names appropriately. To maintain the filing system and adequately houseclean files, schedule times to routinely review the filing system. The times could be uniform from week to week or could be by a once-a-month open time schedule. It is recommended not to let files go unattended for longer than one month.

BUDGETS, RECORDKEEPING, AND ACCOUNTING SYSTEMS

Budgets

Before a discussion of budgeting systems can begin, it must be asserted that the process of budgeting in most camp organizations is fairly simple to understand. So why does the mere mention of the term cause extreme mental distress for many camp administrators? Three reasons stand out. The first is that budgets are predictions and predictions deal with uncertainty. The second is that to do them accurately, budgets take time, thought, and effort. If a camp administrator is not detail oriented, budgeting can be a difficult process. The third is that budgets customarily deal with a very critical and carefully scrutinized organizational resource—money. Money is the one camp resource that draws immediate attention from all camp stakeholders.

While budgeting is focused on financial resources, almost all resources a camp possesses can and should be budgeted. Resources such as camp personnel, materials and supplies, and facility and equipment usage are just a few of the camp items that can be budgeted. This chapter will concentrate on that essential, internal camp resource—money.

Budgeting Defined

The term *budget* when used by a summer sports camp can be defined the following way:

> A budget is (a) the quantitative expression of a proposed plan of action by management for a specific period and (b) an aid to coordinate what needs to be done to implement that plan. A budget generally includes both financial and non-financial aspects of the plan, and it serves as a blueprint for the company to follow in the upcoming period.[2]

Budgets are for a specific time period (ordinarily, one camp season). While they are used for projecting future resource allocation, they are grounded in historical information. In other words, what is spent in a camp's previous budgetary periods will be the foundation for the projections into subsequent budgetary periods. Unfortunately, if the camp is a new venture, this baseline data will not be available.

Budgeting promotes planning and coordination; it enhances performance measurements and corrective actions.

Planning: The budget formalizes and documents managerial plans, clearly communicating objectives to both superiors and subordinates.

Coordination: The budgetary process forces coordination among departments to promote decisions in the best interest of the company as a whole.

Camp Tip

If a camp administrator has never budgeted before, do not think twice about contacting a colleague with experience to request help. Budgeting takes insight as well as practice. Jumping blindly into the budgeting process can have considerable implications for the camp now and in the future.

Performance measurement: Budgets are specific, quantitative representations of management's objectives. Comparing actual results to budgeted expectations provides a way to evaluate performance.

Corrective action: Budgeting provides advanced notice of potential shortages, or other weaknesses in operating plans. . . . Budgeting advises managers of potential problems in time for them to carefully devise effective solutions.[3]

Budgeting and Organizational Goals

Because the ultimate objective of camp management is goal achievement, budgeting and the budgeting process must always have the objectives of the camp in mind. In the simplest terms, budgets are productive tools that will help achieve what the camp wants to accomplish. The worst-case scenario in dealing with budgets is that they are obstacles to achieving goals. "Problems can arise if (1) the budget goal is unachievable (too high), (2) the budget goal is very easy to achieve (too loose), or (3) the budget goals of the business conflict with the objectives of employees (goal conflict)."[4] From a camp administration standpoint, one's budget must be challenging but achievable to maximize the camp's financial resources.

Situational Budgeting

From a camp perspective, budgeting can take two different forms. The first and most difficult occurs when the administrator is the owner of the camp. In this case, one must budget at length and apply detailed accounting procedures to all operations. This situation is similar to corporate accounting. In this type of camp, it is sensible to employ and directly work with an accounting consultant, unless the administrator has a formal accounting and business background. The consultant will help set up all of the camp's projected budgets, recordkeeping, financial statements, and year-end fiscal reports.

The second form of budgeting is the one that is relevant for institutional camps: operating/expense budgeting. This is a budgeting system in which the camp is a part (or *unit*) within the institution overall camp structure. In this case, the process of financial statement generation is completed outside the camp. The administrator is provided with specific limitations within which the camp must operate. In other words, the institution's athletic administration (in a high school, junior college, or senior college) specifies an exact dollar amount for the camp to operate. The projected amount can be divided into predetermined line items or it can be a combined total. In the latter case, the camp administrator determines the amounts for the individual line items.

© Ptlee | Dreamstime.com

Traditional Expense Budgeting

Traditional expense budgeting focuses on the expense side of the income statement (Revenues − Expenses = Net Income/Net Loss). The first step is to identify all of the camp's costs. This concept is not as simple as it seems. A good place to start is with the identification of historical data. Simply put, the expense categories that the camp has had in the past are the foundation for the future projected categories. However, this is not the end of the process. The camp, through planning and goal definition (Chapter 2), has a future-oriented viewpoint that possibly is very different from its current and historical position. In this instance, discover what new expenses need to be defined based on the camp's mission, goals, and direction. The camp administrator needs to think this step through from every possible angle. Look at the camp season completely. While some camp administrators tend to separate their precamp and in-camp expenses, never fail to identify the post-camp expenses.

Once the camp's expense categories have been determined, enter the dollar amounts that are believed to be accurate. As with budget category definitions, historical data is a good place to determine the dollar amount for each expense item. From that starting point, each expense must be looked at individually to determine changes from past camps. In other words, is the camp remaining essentially the same? If so, then the historical expense information is relevant, applicable, and defendable. If the camp's administrator has evaluated and subsequently changed any aspect of the operation, then an increase or decrease in an expense might be warranted.

Zero-Based Budgeting

As previously discussed, budgeting is the administrative responsibility that projects and calculates future camp resource allocations. Budgets provide a tangible framework within which the different components of the camp can operate.

In the traditional approach to budgeting, the manager starts with last year's budget and adds to it (or subtracts from it) according to anticipated needs. . . . Under a zero-based budget, managers are required to justify all budgeted expenditures, not just changes in the budget from the previous year. The baseline is zero rather than last year's budget.[5]

For a camp, zero-based budgeting is considerably more challenging to develop because of the fact that each expense item is considered a new expense and its projected amounts are derived from original data. In other words, while traditional budgets are considered *rollovers,* zero-based budgets stem from primary new budgeting research. If done accurately, zero-based budgets give a truer picture of the financial situation and budgetary projections. A camp administrator needs to determine if the additional accuracy of the zero-based budget justifies the additional time needed to construct it. A possible option is to assemble zero-based budgets every other fiscal period to maintain accuracy of the traditional numbers as well as to keep the camp using up-to-date primary figures.

Budgets as Managerial Controls

Budgets, as managerial control tools, have

four principle purposes: (1) to fine-tune the strategic plan; (2) to help coordinate the activities of the several parts of the organization; (3) to assign responsibility to managers, to authorize the amounts that they are permitted to spend, and to inform them of the performance that is expected of them; and (4) to obtain a commitment that is a basis for evaluating a manager's actual performance.[6]

Considering budgets deal with the most critical and limited resource in a camp (money), all personnel need to have a guide for operating and spending. For this reason, budgets should be continuously monitored by the camp's administrator. A good practice is to keep, either by hand or by computer software, an expense ledger that shows a camp's individual line items. The line items can be broken down into budgeted, actual, and variances. Another ledger technique could be similar to one's personal checkbook, where dates and running balances show the remaining funds as well as when expenses were incurred. Furthermore, if one can accurately maintain running totals, it will give a clear picture of the account. Finally, any major departures from projected to actual spending should be recorded and explained for budget review clarification at the end of the camp season.

Budgets: A Participative Concept

For a camp to have its administrators, coaches, and staff buy into the budget, a participative approach is consistently a strong tactic. Participative budgeting

invites participation in the budget process by personnel at all levels of the organization, not just upper-level managers. Information flows from the bottom up as well as from the top down during the budget preparations.

Because they are directly responsible for meeting budget goals, subordinates can offer more realistic targets. Including them in budget preparation fosters development of a team effort. . . . With participative budgeting, subordinates cannot complain that the budget is management's plan. The budget is instead a self-imposed constraint. Employees can hold no one responsible but themselves if they fail to accomplish the budget objectives they establish.[7]

In addition to having an invested interest in the camp's budget, participative budgeting can generate a new level of focus and energy that can fill all levels of the camp's structure.

Recordkeeping and Accounting Systems

While budgeting systems consider projected future revenues and expenses, recordkeeping and accounting systems record and report camp transactions. Complete explanation of recordkeeping and accounting systems is beyond the scope of this book. As discussed in the budgeting section, designing recordkeeping and accounting systems from the ground up that document camp activities and generate reports is complex and will require someone with knowledge in generally accepted accounting principles, as well as systems development. With that said, there are some considerations that need to be addressed when setting up and using a recordkeeping and accounting system.

- *Ease of use.* This is a major consideration when building an accounting system, especially for recording day-to-day transactions. The system should have step-by-step procedures that can be easily referenced.

- *Comprehensive.* The recordkeeping and accounting system must be able to record and report all areas of the camp's operation. Any system "hiccups" could have a significant impact on accuracy, reporting, and decision making. All staff involved with the system should participate in a detailed review of the system and develop a contingency plan in the event of a system breakdown.

- *Accuracy.* There are two types of errors that need to be eliminated in a camp's accounting and recordkeeping systems: *systemic errors* and *human errors.* Both can have a serious influence on the financial exactness and truth being reported. A systemic error is also known as a *system glitch.* These are errors that are built into the accounting and recordkeeping model that continually happen because of a design oversight, inaccuracy, or lapse. Depending on their implementation, timing, and use, they are often difficult to find and correct. Human errors are centered on the mistakes of the individuals working the system. These can be one-time errors or continuous mistakes. A key way to minimize these is to hire the right personnel to operate the system and train each person on all of the ins and outs of the all-inclusive system. The ideal individual to work the system is detail oriented and careful, someone who understands the value of precision. However, no matter how precise and meticulous the individual, they will need training to completely understand the system. To confirm accuracy, a camp administrator should try to include as many checks and balances within the system as possible. The checks and balances can be either human or automated.

- *Ability to generate timely reports.* At a moment's notice, the camp's system should be able to spit out timely reports. These statements should provide an accurate picture of where the camp is currently. The reports should incorporate account information such as revenues, expenses, assets, liabilities, capital, cash flow, accounts receivable, etc. If accurate, reports produced from accounting and recordkeeping systems help a camp administrator make decisions based on hard financial numbers.

- *Internal controls.* Not only do recordkeeping and accounting systems help the camp administrator make decisions, they also can be used for internal controls. If designed correctly, these systems can perform several functions:
  - supply notices for overspending and waste,
  - provide warnings for low revenue generating areas,
  - furnish alerts for outstanding accounts receivables,
  - convey cautions on payroll variances, and
  - indicate critical capacity use status (both minimum and maximum).

These warnings, if structured within the accounting and recordkeeping system, can prevent substantial operational issues and wasted resources.

- *Consistency.* A compelling consideration for any recordkeeping and accounting system is consistency within the camp. Policies (system rules) and procedures (system how-to's) need to be followed by all recordkeeping and accounting personnel. Any changes—before, during, or after operations—need to be approved and discussed with all parties involved in the system. Short-cuts, while possibly saving time, can have a huge impact on the integrity of the system. A general rule is that consistency in accounting and recordkeeping leads to a higher probability of accuracy.

- *Retention of source documents for audit trail.* The accounting system needs to support a paper trail of original documents. Whether it is purchase orders, invoices, or check stubs, the system must have a way to retrieve original documents promptly. If audited, the accounting system inputs and reports will be the foundation of the evaluation. The original documents will be the supporting backups and verifications of those system inputs and reports.

QuickBooks (QB)

It is not this book's intention to recommend one specific type of accounting software over another. Each camp administrator needs to look at the all-encompassing camp and determine if accounting software is necessary and, if so, which software is the best fit for their operation. With that said, one of the most popular accounting software systems for small businesses in today's market is QuickBooks. The following points are some of the advantages of QuickBooks:

- Different levels of software, from Basic QuickBooks to QuickBooks Pro
- Easy to set up, with a learning curve that is not too steep
- Flexible and easily tailored to any operation
- Able to grow with operation
- Low-cost, prepackaged software
- Adequate to excellent reporting capabilities
- Simple inventory tracking
- Complete security access (password controls and closing date lockouts)
- Internal operations or within QB Cloud system

More information on QuickBooks can be found at: www.quickbooks.com.

ENDNOTES

1. Filing . . . like the beat. . . goes on. . . and on. (2001). *Journal of Accountancy, 192,* 24.
2. Horngren, C. T., Datar, S. M., Foster, G., Rajan, M., & Ittner, C. (2009). *Cost accounting: A managerial emphasis* (13th edition), p. 181. Upper Saddle River, NY: Pearson Prentice Hall.
3. Edmonds, T. P., Tsay, B., Olds, P. R., & Schnieder, N. W. (2009). *Fundamental managerial accounting concepts* (5th edition), p. 305. New York, NY: McGraw-Hill/Irwin.
4. Warren, C. S., Reeve, J. M., & Fess, P. E. (2002). *Accounting* (20th edition), p. 820. Mason, OH: Thompson South-Western.
5. Garrison, R. H., & Noreen, E. W. (2003). *Managerial accounting* (10th edition), p. 380. New York, NY: McGraw-Hill/Irwin.
6. Anthony, R. N., & Govindarajan, V. (2007). *Management control systems* (12th edition), p. 382. New York, NY: McGraw-Hill/Irwin.
7. Edmonds, T. P., Tsay, B., & Olds, P. R. (2008). *Fundamental managerial accounting concepts* (4th edition), p. 276. New York, NY: McGraw-Hill/Irwin.

SECTION IV:

HUMAN RESOURCES

As this section will demonstrate, human resource management is an essential part of any sports camp. The key concept to understand: A camp is only as good as its employees. Their selection, orientation, compensation, and evaluation have an unmistakable impact on the entire camp. The competent use of human resource concepts can fortify a camp. The poor use of human resource systems can spell complete failure.

8

Human Resource Systems

INTRODUCTION

Human resource management (HRM) is best expressed as "designing management systems to ensure that human talent is used effectively to accomplish organizational goals."[1] In the clearest terms, human resource administration for a sports camp is a people-oriented function that greatly affects the productivity and quality of the operation. Productivity can be considered the efficient use of resources to maximize a camp's worth. Undeniably, the most indispensable resource for any camp is its people.

© Godfer | Dreamstime.com

> ### Camp Tip
> Under no circumstances ignore the reality that the people in one's camp are its lifeblood. A camp administrator could never achieve any of the camp's goals if it was not for their dedication and hard work. Focus on the concept of lifeblood of productivity when dealing with the camp's most precious resource: its people.

Human resource management for camps, while having many of the same components of HRM for traditional business organizations, is considered a specialized category of personnel management with distinct conditions. HRM elements for camps that make them unique include the following:

- Camp personnel are hired for a specific time, normally under contracts. Depending on the camp, these limited employments could be for days, weeks, or summer months.

- In most instances, camp personnel regard camp employment as a second, temporary job (not a career position). With a majority of camp personnel, this will not be an issue. However, camp administrators need to recognize that, as with all temporary human resource situations, temporary employees might not be as invested in the camp as full-time employees.

- Camp clinicians must be extraordinarily skilled professionals with wide-ranging experience in the sport they are instructing.

- Administration and staff must be knowledgeable in various camp operations while being able to get up and running on a tight—sometimes almost instant—time frame and being open and adaptable to system changes that could happen at a moment's notice.

- To bolster a camp's brand awareness, high-profile clinicians and coaches could be considered. Unfortunately, celebrated and visible clinicians and coaches for hire often demand salaries that are considerably above market value rates for general clinicians and coaches.

The importance of human resource management for camps cannot be overemphasized. Camps are in a service industry in which the value of the organization's output is precisely related to the expertise and proficiency of the clinicians, staff, and administrators in the operation. While planning and structuring a camp are foundational functions, a camp's human resources are the engine that

- propels performance and productivity,

- has a direct correlation with the camp's future growth,

- determines the overall atmosphere of the entire operation,

- ensures camper safety, and

- supports and promotes the camp through ambassadorship and public relations.

As previously indicated (and it is meaningful to restate), the most valuable aspects of the camp are its people. . . period.

This section will emphasize the administrative function of human resource management. Because these principles are, by and large, relevant to all businesses, situations, and industries, they can be freely tailored to and configured for camps.

Camp Tip

The proverb "you are only as strong as your weakest link" is important to remember when talking about a camp's human resources. Unsurprisingly, the operation will break down at the one person who has not bought into the camp's working goals and philosophy. Forming strong human resource management systems is central to minimize this possibility.

LEGAL ASPECTS OF HRM

The details of human resource law are outside the scope of this text. HR law is a specialty field and is often a lifetime pursuit. It cannot be recommended strongly enough: *All HR systems and processes should be discussed with a competent advisor prior to the camp's inception.* For camp operations within educational institutions, the human resource department is normally a knowledgeable and experienced source of HR knowledge and advisement. For entrepreneurial ventures (stand-alone camps), retaining one or more lawyers with considerable emphasis in employment law can provide a camp with indispensable legal HR protocols and counsel.

In Appendix 8.1, various key human resource laws and acts are presented. While some may not relate to a particular camp, camp administrators should identify, comprehend, and appreciate the legal aspects and responsibilities that go into HRM.

Special Note: It is important that a camp administrator know that there are specific state and local laws and regulations in addition to federal regulations listed in Appendix 8.1. Once again, consult with a HRM expert or legal counsel to review these particular regulations.

One significant human resource legal matter that has changed or been reinterpreted over the past 15-20 years is the classification of whether a person working a camp is an employee or an independent contractor. On the surface, one would assume that temporary contractual employees would be regarded as independent contractors. That assumption could very well be inaccurate. Table 8.1 (derived directly from the Internal Revenue Service's web page) describes some of the criteria for determining if someone is an employee or independent contractor.

Table 8.1. **IRS Rules/Regulations Concerning Employment Classifications**

Common Law Rules

Facts that provide evidence of the degree of control and independence fall into three categories:

1. **Behavioral:** Does the company control or have the right to control what the worker does and how the worker does his or her job?

2. **Financial:** Are the business aspects of the worker's job controlled by the payer? (Controls include things like how worker is paid, whether expenses are reimbursed, who provides tools and supplies, etc.)

3. **Type of Relationship:** Are there written contracts or employee-type benefits (i.e., pension plan, insurance, vacation pay, etc.)? Will the relationship continue and is the work performed a key aspect of the business?

Businesses must weigh all these factors when determining whether a worker is an employee or independent contractor. Some factors may indicate that the worker is an employee, while other factors indicate that the worker is an independent contractor. There is no magic or set number of factors that makes the worker an employee or independent contractor, and no one factor stands alone in making this determination. Also, factors that are relevant in one situation may not be relevant in another.

The keys are to look at the entire relationship, consider the degree or extent of the right to direct and control, and finally, document each of the factors used in coming up with the determination.

Additionally, the IRS has a 20-area examination on whether a person is an independent contractor or an employee. The following 20 points have been established:

1. Must the individual take instructions from your management staff regarding when, where, and how work is to be done?
2. Does the individual receive training from your company?
3. Is the success or continuation of your business somewhat dependent on the type of service provided by the individual?
4. Must the individual personally perform the contracted services?
5. Have you hired, supervised, or paid individuals to assist the worker in completing the project stated in the contract?
6. Is there a continuing relationship between your company and the individual?
7. Must the individual work set hours?
8. Is the individual required to work full time at your company?
9. Is the work performed on company premises?
10. Is the individual required to follow a set sequence or routine in the performance of his work?
11. Must the individual give you reports regarding his or her work?
12. Is the individual paid by the hour, week, or month?
13. Do you reimburse the individual for business and travel expenses?
14. Do you supply the individual with needed tools or materials?
15. Have you made a significant investment in facilities used by the individual to perform services?
16. Is the individual free from suffering a loss or realizing a profit based on his work?
17. Does the individual only perform services for your company?
18. Does the individual limit the availability of his services to the general public?
19. Do you have the right to discharge the individual?
20. May the individual terminate his services at any time?

In general *no* answers to questions 1-16 and yes answers to questions 17-20 indicate an independent contractor. However, a simple majority of *no* answers to questions 1 to 16 and yes answers to questions 17 to 20 does not guarantee independent contractor treatment. Some questions are either irrelevant or of less importance because the answers may apply equally to employees and independent contractors.

Three essential IRS and IRS-related web pages to review with your operation's legal counsel and CPA:

- http://www.irs.gov/Businesses/Small-Businesses-&-Self-Employed/Independent-Contractor-Self-Employed-or-Employee
- http://www.irs.gov/pub/irs-utl/emporind.pdf
- http://www.uncsa.edu/formsprocedures/IRS.htm

One area of caution: There are consequences of treating an employee as an independent contractor. The IRS states that if you classify an employee as an independent contractor and you have no reasonable basis for doing so, you may be held liable for employment taxes for that worker.

From the guidelines and directives specified in Table 8.1, it is critical for a camp administrator to distinguish which clinicians, staff members, and administrators are employees and which are independent contractors.

HIERARCHICAL STRUCTURE AND JOB DESCRIPTIONS

Organizational Charts

A camp's "organizational structure comprises the formal and informal arrangement of tasks, responsibilities, line of authority, and reporting relationships by which the firm is administered."[2] It is a central HRM function to create, prior to hiring summer sports camp personnel, a clear-cut organizational chart. This visual picture will furnish camp stakeholders with a fundamental view of the physical HR make-up of the operation. For summer sports camps, a simple straight-line organizational chart (also known as an *organizational tree*) should be more than sufficient. Figure 8.1 is a basic organizational chart template for a mid-size to large camp enterprise.

Camp Tip

It is once again a reasonable action to evaluate all camp operations (especially the employee-independent contractor issue) with both a lawyer and certified public accountant. These types of precautionary consultations could save a summer sports camp substantial time and money.

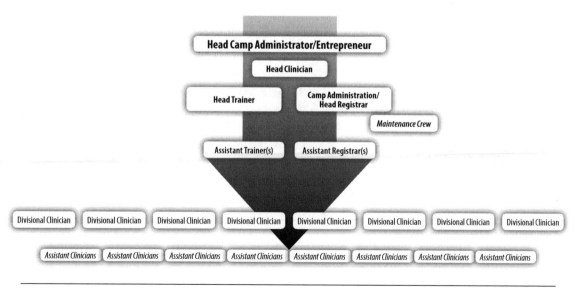

Figure 8.1. **Camp Organizational Chart**

Once the summer sports camp's organizational chart is set, job descriptions for each position should be constructed.

Job Descriptions

Job descriptions are an indispensable component of any organization's management. They provide a summary of the tasks to be performed and state specific requirements for the *position*. The job description serves many different functions:

- It lists minimum performance expectations.
- It discourages uninterested and unqualified individuals from applying.
- It serves as a guideline for selecting and interviewing candidates, and in making your decision on which one to hire.
- It forms the basis of training needs.
- It establishes benchmarks for performance evaluations.
- It may act as evidence against grievances, wrongful termination lawsuits, or claims of discrimination or retaliation.[3]

Table 8.2 provides a core structure for a job description. This template can be readily modified to fit all types of summer sports camp positions. The detail in each job description will be influenced by the complexity of the camp and the complexity of the particular position.

Table 8.2. Core Structure of a Job Description

Job Title

The first division of the job description is the formal and specialized name for the position in the summer sports camp. Other information in this section can include

- job number,
- operational division,
- creation date of job description,
- position in hierarchal scheme—accountability and reporting responsibilities—and
- salary range and compensation package associated with the position.

Occupational Overview

This is the narrative summation of the position and its practical importance in the summer sports camp. While broad in scope, it should give the reader a sense of the details associated with the position.

Job Specifications

The job specifications portion of a job description is the explanation of the primary activities involved in the position. It is advisable to do the following:

- Put all tasks, responsibilities, and functions in descending priority order.
- Bullet tasks, responsibilities, and functions for clarity.
- If possible, place estimated percentages of time for each task, responsibility, and function as they relate to the overall position (totaling 100%).

Knowledge and Ability Requirements for the Position

This segment details the mental and physical aspect mandated to execute the summer sports camp position. Educational minimums, size and weight requirements, and diverse prior sport experience are all possible components of this part.

Head Clinician

While there are many positions that are vital to a camp, the one crucial position is the head clinician. In other words, for a camp to flourish, a critical, leading ingredient is the camp's head clinician. The selection of an individual to fill this position must correspond with the camp's goals, principles, and philosophies. The factors that make up a strong head clinician are difficult to quantify. The qualifications of a dynamic, professional head clinician include

- stimulating intellectual abilities and expert-level, sport-specific knowledge,
- aptitude to recognize and manage change,
- unselfish personality that is camper and clinician centered,
- persuasive and energetic interpersonal communication skills,
- ability to inspire and nurture camp stakeholders,
- proficient in settling conflicts,
- focused decision making, and
- disposition to empower staff and clinicians while holding them accountable, among many others.

Three of these qualities are exceptionally relevant for a camp's head clinician. The first and most important element for every head clinician in any sport is having expert-level, sport-specific knowledge. Simply stated, the head clinician needs to be an encyclopedic reserve of sports knowledge for all participants, employees, and campers.

The second attribute that clearly signals effective head clinicians is their skill in inspiring and encouraging camp participants. To motivate people, from staff to campers, a head clinician must

- tirelessly communicate the summer sports camp's mission and goals,
- support an emotionally stable camp environment,
- establish clear-cut expectations in plain language for stakeholders to abide by,
- objectively critique stakeholders' performance and impart helpful feedback when necessary,
- have a beneficial, hands-on management style, and

- show an unconditional commitment to the camp's short- and long-term goals.

Finally, the third element that contributes to the success of a camp's head clinician is skillful communication on and ability to do the following:

- foster relationships through sincere personal communication,
- engage and motivate people through his or her communication style,
- create a professional persona from his or her skills as a communicator,
- consider his or her audience and select a communication strategy that is suitable for them,
- listen to others and employ that information in making decisions, and
- read nonverbal behaviors, gestures, and mannerisms accurately.

The selection of a talented head clinician is the first step in developing a successful camp. Unfortunately, the selection of the wrong individual could be disastrous, not only for the current camp but any future camps.

© Vitmark | Dreamstime.com

APPENDIX 8.1: SUMMARY OF EQUAL EMPLOYMENT OPPORTUNITY LAWS AND EXECUTIVE ORDERS

LAW/ACT/YEAR	PURPOSE OR INTENT/COVERAGE
Equal Pay Act (1963)	**Purpose:** Prohibits sex-based discrimination in rates of pay for men and women working in the same or similar jobs. **Coverage:** Private employers engaged in commerce or in the production of goods for commerce and with two or more employees; labor organizations.

Title VII, Civil Rights Act (1964/1972)	**Purpose:** Prohibits discrimination based on race, sex, color, religion, or national origin. **Coverage:** Private employers with 15 or more employees for 20 or more weeks per year, institutions, state and local governments, employment agencies, labor unions, and joint labor-management committees
Age Discrimination in Employment Act (1967)	**Purpose:** Prohibits discrimination against individuals who are at least 40 years of age but less than 70. An amendment eliminates mandatory retirement at age 70 for employees of companies with 20 or more employees. **Coverage:** Private employers with 20 or more employees for 20 or more weeks per year, labor organizations, employment agencies, state and local governments, and federal agencies, with some exceptions.
Pregnancy Discrimination Act (1978)	**Purpose:** Requires employers to treat pregnancy just like any other medical condition with regard to fringe benefits and leave policies. **Coverage:** Same as Title VII, Civil Rights Act.
Immigration Reform and Control Act (1986)	**Purpose:** Prohibits hiring of illegal aliens. **Coverage:** Any individual or company.
Americans with Disabilities Act (1990)	**Purpose:** Increase access to services and jobs for disabled workers. **Coverage:** Private employers with 15 or more employees.
Older Workers Benefit Protection Act (1990)	**Purpose:** Protects employees over 40 years of age in regard to fringe benefits and gives employees time to consider an early retirement offer. **Coverage:** Same as Age Discrimination Employment Act.
Civil Rights Act (1991)	**Purpose:** Permits women, persons with disabilities, and persons who are religious minorities to have a jury trial and sue for punitive damages if they can prove intentional hiring and workplace discrimination. Also requires companies to provide evidence that the business practice that led to the discrimination was not discriminatory but was job related for the position in question and consistent with business necessity. **Coverage:** Private employers with 15 or more employees.
Family and Medical Leave Act (1993)	**Purpose:** Enables qualified employees to take prolonged unpaid leave for family and health-related reasons without fear of losing their jobs. **Coverage:** Private employers with 15 or more employees.[4]

ENDNOTES

1. Mathis, R. L., & Nkomo, S. M. (2008). *Applications in human resources,* p. 450. Mason, OH: Cengage Learning.

2. Thompson, A. A., Peteraf, M. A., Strickland, A. J., & Gamble, J. E. (2014). *Crafting and executing strategy: The quest for competitive advantage: Concepts and cases* (19th edition), p. 302. New York, NY: McGraw-Hill/Irwin.

3. Muller, M. (2012). *Legal side of HR practice,* p. 23. New York, NY: AMACOM Self-Study.

4. Byars, L. L., & Rue L. W. (2011). *Human resource management* (10th edition), p. 33. New York, NY: McGraw-Hill/Irwin.

CHAPTER 8

Human Resource Management

STAFFING SYSTEMS

A camp administrator's skillful use of staffing systems is related to acquiring the precise number and highest qualified clinicians, administrators, staff, and medical personnel. This chapter analyzes the human resource concepts of demand shift analysis, HR planning, and recruitment and selection.

Demand Shift Analysis

When starting a review of staffing, one must first examine the camp's demand for human resources and the external factors that influence that demand. External factor questions that can affect human resource demands include the following:

- How will a shift in the local, regional, or national economies affect our camp? Since camps rely on unrestricted income for funding, will an economic change in our operating community result in a financial change in our internal camp system? In turn, will this shift in our financial situation affect our hiring decisions?

- Is our camp considered socially responsible in its hiring and recruitment? What does our governing athletic association state about camp recruitment and hiring?

- Will we be able to increase our camp's personnel through effective use of technology?

- What are our competitors doing in terms of recruitment and hiring? Are they growing or downsizing? Are they focusing their human resource efforts on a certain individual with particular strengths and areas of expertise?

These are just a few of the questions that could be asked when looking at the outside factors that can impact a summer sports camp's staffing demands. It should be noted that whenever one is examining any external environmental element that could affect a camp, this should be done not only from a human resource perspective, but in all areas of operation. Examine each factor as an opportunity or a threat. If it is an opportunity, strategize how to exploit it. If the environmental element is a threat, minimize and defend against it.

Internal elements that might shift a camp's demand for personnel are administration forces and the current workforce. These internal factors need continuous oversight and management. Administration elements such as a camp's plan, budget and forecasted projections, new training services, and job designs are all explicit elements that have a direct relationship with human resource needs.

Budgeting and forecasting are the most obvious and immediate causes for hiring clinicians, administrators, and staff. Budgeting and forecasting place into focus what a camp can spend and what it projects to expense and earn in the future. They determine the camp's size, operational limits, equipment and facilities, and human resource limitations.

Another summer sports camp strategy is new ventures. If planned properly, not only will these changes have goals and structure, but they will also have human resource demands within specific timeframes. New services and training sessions are directly related to the camp plan and should be included within that document.

The last of the internal camp elements that affect human resource demand for a camp is *job design*. Job design refers to the initial development of positions in a new camp or the restructuring of positions in an ongoing camp. Either way, new job designs and descriptions typically mean a fundamental change in internal human resource demands for the camp.

Another element that might shift human resource demand is the summer sports camp's current workforce. Camp administrators should see the other administrators, coaches, and staff as a workforce. This workforce must be thought of as a flexible, flowing component of an operation that could change daily. Some changes can be anticipated and planned for, such as, for example, a scheduled leave of absence. However, other changes might not be so easy to predict. Sudden and critical demand can arise from an unforeseen resignation, employment termination, or severe illness and injury. To offset sudden shifts in a camp's human resource demands, a camp will need to have in place a well-defined staffing system.

Once a need for human resources has been determined through a demand analysis, a camp administrator must apply a step-by-step staffing strategy. Staffing strategies for clinicians, administrators, and staff members for camps can be separated into three types: HR manpower planning, recruiting, and selection.

> **Camp Tip**
>
> Clarifying employment needs for an established, ongoing summer sports camp is challenging. It is even more difficult for new summer sports camp ventures. The key is to examine the camp's capacity and the targeted ratio of instructors to participants. For example, if the maximum number of campers a facility can safely and effectively instruct is 100 and the instructional philosophy of the summer sports camp is to have a clinician-to-participant ratio of 10 to 1 (while preserving quality expectations), then the highest number of clinicians would be 10. From there, determine actual hires on projections, always knowing that the camp will not require more than 10 clinicians or instructors at any one time.

HR Manpower Planning

HR manpower planning, which is comparable to human resource demand planning, but more specific and narrowly defined, is

> the process of anticipating and making provisions for the movement of people into, within, and out of an organization. Its purpose is to deploy these resources as effectively as possible, where and when they are needed, in order to accomplish the organization's goals.[1]

Figure 9.1 outlines the step-by-step process for manpower planning in summer sports camps.

Step 1
From the summer sports camp plan, lay out and revisit all of the projected goals and actions for the entire enterprise.

Step 2
Re-examine all of the departments and job positions in the summer sports camp structure. Each job should have a comprehensive list of all current and future duties and responsibilities.

Step 3
Use each individual job list of duties and responsibilities to analyze what human resource skills, education, and experience each duty and responsibility requires (both now and in the future). This is commonly known as the job analysis process.

Step 4
Complete a current skills inventory for each person in those job positions. The skills inventory will examine the individual's ability to fulfill the job duties and responsibilities based on Step 3's analysis of the skills, education, and experience required to perform the summer sports camp's job duties and responsibilities.

Step 5
The concluding step is to construct an action plan. This action plan is used to align the goals and objectives of the summer sports camp with the current human resource asset of the camp.

Figure 9.1. **Manpower/Human Resource Planning for Summer Sports Camps**

The camp's administrator needs to carefully analyze both long-term goals, which are future oriented by nature, and short-term objectives, which call for more immediate actions. One must prioritize which of these goals (short term and action oriented or long term and future oriented) are critical and in need of quality clinicians, administrators, or staff members. Two scenarios may surface from this process. The first is that the summer sports camp's existing manpower is sufficient for its future goals and direction. In this case, the camp administrator might need to adjust job responsibilities and workloads, but the camp's personnel will remain essentially the same. The second scenario is that the camp's manpower needs are lacking and will require additional personnel to attain the future camp objectives.

Manpower planning for the camps can be accomplished simply through a diagram known as a depth chart. A depth chart is a flexible diagram that lists the positions in the camp and the people in each position. How the camp administrator designs the graph is entirely subjective. One possible design is as follows:

1. Across the topmost section of the chart, list the positions in the summer sports camp.

2. Arrange the current camp personnel under each category in order of significance and value. If there are clinicians, administrators, or staff members who are multi-skilled, classify and index them under their primary area.

3. After placing camp personnel in descending order, highlight any open positions and targeted new hires.

This diagram will furnish the camp administrator with a visual picture of future recruiting requirements as well as determine where each clinician, administrator, and staff member is currently situated in the camp. Always consider this document a flexible chart. Camp personnel can progress up and down as their abilities increase or decrease.

Camp Tip

Depth charts can have two valuable purposes in a summer sports camp. The first and most obvious is that they evaluate the open positions and turnover succession of the camp. The second is that they can be used as motivational tools. Some clinicians, administrators, and staff members might not be content with where they lie in the camp's depth chart. This could encourage them to increase their productivity levels and commitment to the camp.

Recruiting and Selecting

After HR manpower planning has been outlined and there is a definite human resource need for the summer sports camp, the next logical procedure in staffing is recruiting. "Recruiting is the process of developing a pool of qualified applicants who are interested in working for the organization and from which the organization might reasonably select the best individual or individuals to hire for employment."[2]

Sources of Camp Personnel

There are two resources for attaining a pool of qualified applicants: internal sources (promotion from within) and external sources.

Internal sources for camp personnel can include

- current clinicians, administrators, and staff members already in the camp program;
- potential employees recommended by current camp personnel; and
- former, rehirable camp employees.

External sources for summer sports camp personnel can include

- media advertising in wide-ranging or targeted media (newspapers, trade publications, radio, TV, etc.);
- college and university graduates with a focus in coaching, sport management, coaching education, or a concentrated sports-level knowledge;
- networking sources in the particular sport in which the summer sports camp operates; and
- other external sources such as walk-ins and word-of-mouth contacts.

Which source a camp administrator selects hinges on the recruiting situation as well as the benefits and drawbacks of each method. Table 9.1 is a bullet point list of the benefits and drawbacks of internal and external recruiting.

Table 9.1. Internal and External Recruiting Benefits and Drawbacks

Internal Recruiting Benefits

- Internal recruiting is a motivational tool for current camp personnel. For example, a group clinician is going to execute his or her current position to the best of his or her ability if he or she knows the camp has a divisional clinician position available.
- There is a reduced amount of risk with internal sources. Simply put, a camp administrator is already, through a working relationship, familiar with the talent and potential of a present camp employee. That individual is an established quantity.
- The learning curve, which is characterized as the time an employee takes to become proficient in his or her position, isn't as steep for a current camp member. While the individual being promoted will need to develop additional skills and learning in his or her new position, he or she is already accustomed to and familiar with the camp's systems, internal policies and procedures, and personnel.
- Promotion within leads to a cascading situation throughout the entire summer sports camp operation. For example, if a head clinician position is filled by a current camp divisional clinician, that divisional clinician's position could be filled by a group clinician. In turn, that position could be filled by an assistant clinician. *Continued*

Table 9.1. **Internal and External Recruiting Benefits and Drawbacks** *(continued)*

Internal Recruiting Drawbacks

- The first negative aspect associated with internal recruiting relates to what most human resource theorists call inbreeding of ideas. Employees who are promoted from within a camp could either be set in their ways or so programmed by long-term habit that they do not envision other methods of completing tasks.

- If there is more than one eligible candidate for an open position, promotion from within can lead to an exceptionally competitive work environment. Some would argue that this internal competitiveness drives individuals to function better while others would say that it breaks up the cohesiveness of the team atmosphere.

- If the camp has an open position with several qualified candidates, the individual members not acquiring the open position could have irreparable morale- and employment-related issues in the future.

External Recruiting Benefits

- Bringing someone in from the outside, external recruiting, has an overriding benefit of infusing the summer sports camp with innovative ideas, work processes and procedures, novel talents and skills, and fresh energy.

- External recruiting, with a suitable pool of candidates, can bring attention to a camp.

- An external recruit is not entangled in the internal camp politics. The candidate can bring about more substantive change by being involved less.

External Recruiting Drawbacks

- The first and possibly most internally damaging side effect of external recruiting is the existing camp members' perception of how they were stepped over or given false hope of being promoted. This scenario can be especially harmful with long-term personnel who have been dedicated to the camp.

- The expenses associated with external recruiting are a great deal higher than internal promotion. Additionally, while internal promotion can take literally days or even minutes, external recruiting can take weeks and, conceivably, months.

- There is more risk in external recruiting than internal. While recruiting and selection have logical step-by-step processes to follow, there are no assurances that the selection of an external recruit will be successful.

- An external recruit not only has a steeper learning curve for the position but an overall learning curve for the summer sports camp. This camp learning curve adds time and a shortfall of productivity until the newly hired camp employee understands the camp's operating systems.

Selection Process

Now that the sources have been clarified, the next stage is the selection process. The selection process, which can be terminated at any time, customarily proceeds as follows:

Phase One. Phase one consists of applications and questionnaires and a review of résumés. These two types of HR tools are recognized techniques for gathering relevant information regarding a specific individual. The design of applications and questionnaires is limited by legal boundaries. Employment applications must conform to all Equal Employment Opportunity Commission and Privacy Information Act requirements. Application forms are universally used and can take on different formats.

Properly prepared, the application form serves four purposes:

- It is a record of the applicant's desire to obtain the position.
- It provides the interviewer with a profile of the applicant that can be used during the interview.
- It is a basic employee record for applicants who are hired.
- It can be used for research on the effectiveness of the selection process.[3]

Camp Tip

Some application and questionnaire categories are more important in the selection of a camp employee than others. Depending on the volume of applications and questionnaires received, a camp administrator must prioritize which categories to review for an applicant's camp suitability. In other words, in critical categories, establish ranges that must be met for a candidate to be considered. This technique can eliminate hours of tedious review.

Phase Two. Phase two consists of an informal preliminary interview. It is the basic assessment of the talent of a potential camp employee. It can be as informal as the administrator and other staff members verbally assessing a candidate's qualifications or as formal as charting detailed selection criteria and measuring the results.

Phase Three. Phase three consists of face-to-face conferences. The camp administrator initiates this meeting through an in-depth interview. The intensity and format of the interview is determined by the significance and gravity of the position in the camp's operating scheme. For example, for head clinicians, face-to-face meetings can be on campus, one on one, in a group interviewing session, etc.

There is characteristically one way for a camp administrator to become a skillful interviewer—by doing interviews. It takes time and practice. However, there are some fundamental areas that can help an individual become a more accomplished interviewer.

Area 1: A camp administrator must carefully prepare for each and every interview. Interview preparation is a mental state. The mental preparation for an interview involves clearing one's mind of other distractions so absolute attention can be given to the candidate being interviewed. Interviewing components can encompass times and locations, a thorough examination of each candidate's credentials and history, and pre-established questions.

Area 2: The second area in interviewing is the actual interview.

Objectives of interviewing include narrowing the search for an employee by assessing each candidate's interpersonal and communication skills, seeing whether the supervisor and employee are comfortable with each other, and learning details about information the candidate has provided on the application or resume. In addition, each candidate has an opportunity to learn about the organization, which helps him or her make a decision about accepting a job offer.[4]

Interview

The actual interview can have a variety of formats and participants. A camp administrator can conduct the interview over a meal, with camp supervisors, in his or her office, or in a separate conference area. Additionally, a camp administrator can ask pre-established questions that have predetermined answers or use open-ended questions that produce more probing reactions.

Special significant notation: It is important that a camp administrator avoid, at all costs, questions that are illegal and discriminatory. Prior to interviewing, it is strongly advised to analyze areas and questions that can or cannot be asked during an interview. Sources for this type of information are human resource departments, human resource textbooks, and legal counsel.

Area 3: Post-interview assessment is the last area in interviewing. After the conclusion of the interview (or interviews), a camp administrator needs to unemotionally examine all the facts and data gathered during the entire selection process. Items such as notes taken during interviews, comments given by other interview participants, responses to questions asked, and overall behavior of individuals are just some of the elements a camp administrator must evaluate.

Camp Tip

Before conducting a face-to-face interview with a potential camp employee, prepare a list of appropriate questions that will prioritize information needed to evaluate the candidate. Outline the presentation but encourage open dialog. Keep in mind that the more one practices interviewing, the better one will become at it. Another critical aspect of interviewing is to avoid letting the conversation go too far out on indirect topics. These interviewing departures will lead the conversations to irrelevant subjects instead of camp operations and the interviewee's fit within those operations.

Phase Four. Phase four consists of employment reference checks. This step in the selection process is consistently disregarded, but is crucial in confirming the character of the potential employee. The camp administrator should have a slate of questions ready for all reference calls.

Margie Arnold, Regina Glover, and Cheryl Beeler, in their textbook, *Human Resource Management in Recreation, Sport, and Leisure Services,* discuss the importance of verifying information in the following passage:

> Do not assume all the information you receive from applicants is true. Believe it or not, major studies have found that from one-third to one-half of all resumes contain overstated, misleading, and/or false information, intentional omissions, and blatant errors. . . . It is the agency's responsibility to properly screen candidates and this includes verifying certifications and other job requirements.[5]

Phase Five. Phase five consists of negotiations and hiring. After all the useful information has been collected and employment and personal references checked, the decision is made to offer the position contingent on a background check.

HUMAN RESOURCE BACKGROUND CHECKS. Due to the make-up of summer sports camps, all camp administrators, clinicians, and staff with direct interaction with youth participants should have comprehensive background checks. The process is as follows:

1. A preliminary offer of employment is made and a detailed consent form is completed by the future employee. At this point, it should be made clear that all employment offers are contingent upon successful completion of a background check.

2. The consent form, which features all applicable information for a background check, is sent electronically or by traditional mail to an independent, authorized third party. At this point, fingerprint checks are also a sensible precaution.

3. The prospective employee, through an independent, authorized third party, submits to a drug screening test. Any irregularities in screening results must be clarified and have a doctor's supporting documentation.

4. Camp administrators make any subsequent reference calls to verify a prospective employee's information and character.

Under no circumstances should an individual be allowed to work a summer sports camp until their employment file and background checks have been fulfilled. A general turnaround time for background checks and drug screening by independent agencies is normally 48-72 hours. All background check practices should be examined by the organization's human resources professionals and legal counsel.

Two rules must always be applied to securing additional administrators, clinicians, and staff members. The first standard is to always convey the truth in all recruiting practices, no matter how much the camp might desire or need a particular individual. The second principal is to never "negative recruit" against another sports camp for administrators, clinicians, and staff. Negative recruiting is basically

Camp Tip

Before a negotiation of any kind, evaluate which elements are negotiable and which are not. Negotiations, by their very nature, are cooperative meetings. However, one needs to declare up front which items in the meeting are open for discussion and which items are deal breakers. Not only will a camp administrator avoid personnel errors by using this technique, he or she will set the atmosphere of the interview and have total control of the negotiation.

identifying other competitors for a potential camp employee and expressing disapproving remarks about their administration, coaches, and overall camp. Violating these basic rules will always come back to haunt the summer sports camp one is trying to build and maintain.

SUMMER CAMP ORIENTATION AND TRAINING

After going through the demanding recruiting and selection process, the camp administrator has acquired who he or she believes is the ideal, best-suited candidate. The new member's first camp impressions are the most significant component in determining the length and productivity of the individual's tenure. The initial hours and days set the tone for the individual on what work ethics, policies and procedures, and overall culture exists in the camp. A professional, appropriately structured orientation and training program is key to achieving the right atmosphere. Conversely, a haphazard and incomplete orientation and training program can have a destructive and often long-term influence on the new hire.

> New employee orientation can be a daunting challenge for employers. New hires are often inundated with forms, procedures, and people but lack a strong sense of the business and operations in which they have begun work. While new-hire orientation programs can attempt to assist new employees in their transition into the workplace, if the programs were not developed in tandem with any strategic objectives or in concert with other HR programs and/or critical operational areas of the organization, they often don't have a significant impact on the new hire's ability to fully understand the entire organization and his or her place in it.[6]

The training for instructional personnel is extremely different from training a full-time athletic program employee. The training often consists of an orientation with several characteristics:

- reviews all facilities,
- outlines time sessions,
- discusses practice and instructional plans, and
- provides a general rundown of principal operational elements.

Due to limited time, instructional personnel must be equipped to instantly assume camp duties. They must already have sport-specialized expertise and teaching abilities prior to arriving and working at the camp.

Once again, the most far-reaching instructional position in a summer sports camp is the head clinician. This individual should be accountable for the following camp orientation and training elements:

- precamp lesson plans,
- demonstration teaching,
- drills and practice activities,

- breaks and rest periods that include warm-up and cool-down routines,
- staff assignment and supervision,
- medical staff assignments and supervision,
- participant safety during instructional activities, and
- all activities related to instruction.

There are two areas when discussing summer sports camp orientation and training. The first relates to attention to detail. Never assume that a camp employee knows something that may be obvious to you or other long-time camp personnel. These assumptions could have drastic results in the future. Second, the recency theory, which states that humans recall more information closer to an activity, should be applied. Orientation and training should be conducted within a few days, if not sooner, of a camp's launch.

Table 9.2 is a basic compilation of possible camp orientation areas. It is up to each camp administrator to choose which component to emphasize.

REWARDS AND COMPENSATION

As mentioned throughout this book, the most valuable asset in a camp is its people. To promote a quality camp atmosphere, the goal should be to hire the most competent clinicians, staff, and administrators. With that said, their compensation should correspond to and surpass their expectations, as long as resources and camp revenues allow. "The purpose of reward systems includes attracting and retaining good employees, motivating performance, encouraging skill development, fostering organizational culture, and fostering organizational structure."[7]

Compensation for individual contractual employees should be as uncomplicated and complete as possible. Contracts and letters of agreement must detail responsibilities, time schedules, compensation, payment schedules, and housing and food provisions, if applicable. All contracts and letters of agreement must be agreed to and signed while being permanently retained in camp files. In addition to contracts and letters of agreement, job descriptions should also be approved and signed.

Intrinsic and Extrinsic Rewards

When discussing the human resource elements involved in rewards and compensation, a camp

> **Camp Tip**
>
> Most camps within an athletic organization utilize the sport's head or associate head coach as the head clinician. Knowledge, competence, and experience are musts when contracting an external head clinician. The position is far too important for a camp to have an untested and inexperienced individual.

Table 9.2. Orientation/Training Items for a Summer Sports Camp

Introduction and Greeting from All Camp Administrators and Head Clinician

Overview of the Camp Plan

Review of the Camps Policies and Procedures

Detailed Diagram of All Athletic, Medical, Residential, and Training Facilities Being Used by Summer Sports Camp

Physical Tour of the Entire Camp

Head Clinicians Instruction System to Include:
- precamp lesson plans
- demonstration teaching
- drills and practice activities
- breaks and rest periods
- cross-training activities
- warm-up and cool-down routines

Review of Camp Personnel Evaluations, Compensation Policies, and General HR Items

Hierarchical Chart and Group Assignments

Distribution of Job Descriptions

Group Breakout Sessions

Open Q & A Session

Distribution of Camp Personnel Merchandise

administrator must understand the concepts of intrinsic and extrinsic rewards and benefits. Intrinsic rewards, or internally motivated behavior

> is performed for its own sake; the source of motivation is actually performing the behavior, and motivation comes from doing the work itself. Many managers are intrinsically motivated; they derive a sense of accomplishment and achievement from helping the organization to achieve its goals and gain a competitive advantage. . . . [E]xtrinsically motivated behavior is behavior that is performed to acquire material or social rewards or to avoid punishment; the source of motivation is the consequences of the behavior, not the behavior itself.[8]

Intrinsically motivated rewards and behavior differs from individual to individual. Each camp employee will have different feelings of accomplishment when completing a task. A major function of the interview process is to find individuals who have a strong level of intrinsic/internal motivation to complete the duties of the position for which they are hired.

Extrinsic/external rewards, which are rewards and compensation such as salary and job-related perks, are dictated by the financial status of the camp, the job position, and the qualifications of the individual. Contrary to other human resource systems, compensation will also be determined by the rules regarding professionalism. Administrators, coaches, and staff members, however, can qualify for the same compensation rewards as any other business employee. Their compensation can include salaries or hourly wages, commissions, and performance bonuses. In other words, the level and detail of the camp's employee compensation package is determined by the camp's environment and specific situation.

If a camp employee is an amateur athlete, the rules of amateurism and the sport's governing body under which compensation for athletes is strictly controlled will apply. Colleges have a compensation system supported by scholarships. The governing organizations (NCAA, NAIA, NJCAA, etc.) have established a very detailed set of rules regarding outside employment. Junior Olympic levels as well as high school programs are also strictly bound by the rules of amateurism for athletes.

Performance Bonus Systems and Camp Perks

If a camp has the financial ability, strong consideration should be given to the development and implementation of a performance-based bonus system. Bonus systems can be centered on individual performance, group achievement, camp objectives met, or a combination of all three. Constructing a sound, structured, and fair bonus (pay-for-performance) system initially takes time to develop and implement. Consideration must be given to the fact that some job performances are difficult to measure. Furthermore, camp administrators must evaluate performance goals and decide which elements warrant pay-for-performance measures. A fair bonus system can not only boost performance and tangible results, but camp morale can be substantially increased. Often, the external reward becomes secondary to the internal feeling of recognition for a job well done.

Supplying camp personnel with extra perks can help retain them for future camps:

- travel to and from camp with per diem or direct reimbursement;
- lodging on or off campus—if on campus as a responsibility of overnight camper supervision, additional compensation should be included;
- camp merchandise such as camp logo shirts, shoes, promotional materials, etc.;
- hospitality table for precamp breakfast, during camp breaks, and post-camp meals;
- insurance coverage for the duration of camp sessions—in most cases, this should be a requirement rather than a perk;
- recreational activities and accessibility to workout facilities; and
- camp meal or banquet at the end of all sessions.

The welfare of employees should be prioritized when developing a camp's structure. Safety issues should be collectively examined by all summer sports camp personnel, and all concerns should be addressed immediately. As a part of their camp compensation, all camp personnel should be able to purchase—or be supplied free—summer camp insurance.

POST-CAMP EVALUATIONS

The primary basis behind the evaluation of summer sports camp employees is to supply feedback, evaluate goals, and improve future productivity. The following points should be utilized when forming an employee evaluation structure.

1. Performance evaluation should include self-evaluation.
2. Performance evaluation should be intended to aid in the development of dedicated, performing, growing individuals.
3. Evaluation is in part subjective.
4. "No evaluation" is not an option.
5. When an evaluation process is perceived as relevant, fair, and effective, people will tend to use it responsibly. When it is not, people will still do something, but they may not feel that it is a compelling responsibility.
6. Performance evaluation is a formal process.[9]

While the short-term nature of camp employment might influence an administrator to avoid performance evaluations, this would be a mistake, especially if the camp is to be an annual enterprise. Not only do they provide a written record of employment performance, which could be a foundation for future employment, they also are a positive tool for personal development.

Camp Tip

To reduce conflicts, emphasize to all camp employees that compensation packages are confidential. All related conversations will be between the camp administrator and the individual, not among one another.

While there are numerous evaluation techniques available for a camp administrator (see Appendix 9.1 for MBOs and 360 Degree Evaluations), the basic numerical rating scale (as presented in Figure 9.2) could be the simplest and most appropriate to employ.

From the example in Figure 9.2, the following can be derived about numerical rating scales:

Camp Tip

No matter what performance evaluation tool used, it should be dated and signed by all parties: employee, direct supervisor, head clinician, and camp administrator.

- easy to construct and implement,

- able to be tailored to specific camp operations,

- has subjective and objective performance measures, and

- can provide an itemized or overall performance rating.

Table 9.3 presents some of the possible categories to be incorporated into a numerical rating scale performance evaluation for a summer sports camp.

Figure 9.2. **Numerical Rating Scale Illustration**

Item: Team Work and Cooperation

Exceptional	Exceeds Expectations	Meets Expectations	Improvement Needed	Not Acceptable
5	4	3	2	1

Comments: _____

Table 9.3. **Potential Numerical Rating Scale Categories**

Teamwork/Cooperation	Leadership
Job/Sport Knowledge	Motivation and Enthusiasm
Ability to Communicate to Groups	Emotional Intelligence
Interpersonal Communication	Attendance and Punctuality
Initiative	Administrative Skills
Creativity and Decision Making	Customer/Camper Relations
Productivity and Results	Overall

APPENDIX 9.1: PERFORMANCE EVALUATIONS: MBOs (MANAGEMENT BY OBJECTIVES) AND 360 EVALUATIONS

MBO assessments are a more cooperative, motivational, and constructive method of employee evaluations than the traditional, one-way critical judgment analysis.

The MBO process is as follows:

1. **Job review and agreement.** The employee and the supervisor review the job description and the key activities that constitute the employee's job. The idea is to agree on the exact make-up of the job.

2. **Development of performance standards.** Together, the employee and his or her supervisor develop specific standards of performance and determine a satisfactory level of performance that is specific and measurable.

3. **Setting of objectives.** Together, the employee and the supervisor establish objectives that are realistically attainable.

4. **Continuing performance discussions.** The employee and the supervisor use the objectives as a basis for continuing discussion about the employee's performance. Although a formal review session may be scheduled, the employee and the supervisor do not necessarily wait until the appointed time to discuss performance. Objectives are mutually modified as warranted.[10]

This process is a continual and repeating system. From the four-step process, a key term must be emphasized: *mutual.* This collaborative type of evaluation process is in the best interest of the employee and summer sports camp. From the point of view of the employee, the system is good because it supports individuals with clear objectives that have been established with their own input. Furthermore, camp administrators will find that this method strengthens employee confidence and levels of motivation, it creates strong lines of communication, and it cultivates teamwork.

Two other key points should be emphasized in employing MBO evaluations. Remember that evaluations are joint efforts. At first, the direct supervisor might have to draw out the program member in the partnership aspects of clarifying objectives. It should also be clear that the employee is accountable for his or her performance. The second key point is that there should be occasional checkpoints. These checkpoints can be in the form of formal meetings or informal updates.

Special Note: Often, the most difficult aspect of an MBO evaluation is drawing out the employees so that they contribute to the process. To have them collaborate in their own productivity and camp future, uncover what motivates them. Start the MBO process there in order to get them invested into all aspects of their position. Then explain to them the critical importance of items that might not be individual motivators.

360-Degree Evaluations

An evaluation method that has gained momentum in the business world and can be adopted by camps is called a *360-degree performance evaluation*. It differs from traditional, one-way performance assessments in that an individual is given work-related performance evaluations from all possible people the individual works with and for (e.g., peers, supervisors, campers). Additionally, a true 360-degree evaluation also examines the individual's own assessment of how he or she performed.

There are three key assumptions on which 360-degree feedback is based:

1. Multiple viewpoints from multiple sources will produce a more accurate picture of one's strengths and weaknesses than would a single reviewer's evaluation;

2. The act of comparing one's own self-perception with others' perception will lead to enhanced self-awareness, and greater self-awareness is a good thing;

3. People who are effective at what they do will have self-perceptions that match others' perception of them fairly closely.[11]

All performance assessments systems have noticeable drawbacks. The drawbacks of the 360-degree system are as follows:

- Personalities can be overemphasized. In other words, the individual's actual performance could become secondary if the evaluators emphasize one's likeability rather than skill and productivity.

- If the peer environment in a camp is competitive, 360-degree evaluations will likely provide an incorrect picture of an individual's work quality and productivity.

- A 360-degree evaluation form needs to be constructed separately for each evaluation group. The evaluation criteria that a supervisor might feel are important might not necessarily be what a subordinate is concerned with.

- An individual's self-assessment might not be based on reality.

- It takes time to compile 360-degree evaluations and number-crunch the accumulated data from all of the sources.

APPENDIX 9.2: DISCIPLINARY SYSTEM

Stage 1: Oral/Verbal Warnings

Level 1: Oral/Verbal Warning (No Documentation)
This form of warning is for lesser/minor camp offenses. No follow-up or written documentation is associated with this type of warning.

Level 2: Oral/Verbal Warning (Documentation)
This disciplinary discussion requires some manner of supporting written documentation. It should be kept as a permanent record in the camp personnel file.

Stage 2: Written Warnings

Level 1: Written Warning (Internal Documentation)

This phase and intensity of disciplinary action has a formal, signed form retained in the camp's personnel file. It should be discussed at an official meeting with other camp members in attendance. All who participate (including the violator) should sign off on the document.

Level 2: Written Warning (Internal and External Documentation)

This level of written warning is the same as Level 1 except that the written portion is maintained not only inside the camp's personnel file, but also in the overall organization's records. Because of the gravity of this violation, it is advisable to have a departmental administrator present to observe the meeting.

Stage 3: Suspensions/Dismissals

Level 1: Suspensions

This critical disciplinary situation involves the camp employee receiving a suspension from all camp activities. The length of the suspension could be predetermined or could be set through an advisory meeting with the organization's administration. All suspensions must be entirely documented with the full knowledge and support of all camp administrators. The camp member can bring in outside counsel if so desired.

Level 2: Dismissal

This terminal stage involves the camp employee's permanent discharge or release from all camp activities and functions. Because of the severity of this type of response to a camp violation, all parties should be well represented. Once again, comprehensive documentation is mandatory. It is also prudent to videotape the dismissal conference.

APPENDIX 9.3: GRIEVANCE SYSTEM

Step 1

The camp employee being disciplined must notify all relevant parties (camp administrators) in writing that he or she is contesting a disciplinary action and must describe his or her side of the disciplinary issue.

Step 2

The camp administration will coordinate a timely grievance meeting with internal camp personnel (as well as persons outside the camp) to review the legitimacy of the individual's claim. Additionally, the camp administration will issue a written confirmation to the disciplined individual stating that a grievance committee meeting will convene.

Step 3

If the committee feels that the individual's situation warrants further attention, an official hearing will be called. If the committee judges the discipline to be in accordance with camp policies and procedures, a written notification will be issued to the camp member detailing the findings.

Step 4

The official meeting convenes with all relevant parties and witnesses. It is strongly recommended that the meeting be recorded by an independent third party.

Step 5

After the official meeting, the committee will make its final decision concerning the disciplinary action. The individual will be informed in writing (and in a timely manner) of the final decision.

ENDNOTES

1. Bohlander, G., Snell, S., & Sherman, A. (2001). *Managing human resources,* p. 122. Cincinnati, OH: South-Western Publishing.
2. DeNisi, A. S., & Griffin, R. W. (2001). *Human resource management,* p. 170. Boston, MA: Houghton Mifflin.
3. Mathis, R. L., & Nkomo, S. M. (2008). *Applications in human resources,* p. 215. Mason, OH: Cengage Learning.
4. Certo, S. (2008). *Supervision: Concepts and skill building* (6th edition), p. 419. New York, NY: McGraw-Hill/Irwin.
5. Arnold, M., Glover, R., & Beeler, C. (2012). *Human resource management in recreation, sport, and leisure services,* p. 95. State College, PA: Venture Publishing.
6. Mello, & Schaffer. (2008). *Advanced human resource management,* pp. 244-245. Mason, OH: Cengage Learning.
7. Chelladurai, P. (2006). *Human resource management in sport and recreation* (2nd edition), p. 233. Champaign, IL: Human Kinetics.
8. Jones, G. R., & George, J. M. (2006). *Contemporary management* (4th edition), pp. 457-458. New York, NY: McGraw-Hill/Irwin.
9. Yow, D., Migliore, R. H., Bowden, W. W., Stevens, R. E., & Loudon, D. L. (2000). *Strategic planning for collegiate athletics,* p. 85. New York, NY: Haworth Half-Court Press.
10. Mathis, R. L., & Nkomo, S. M. (2008). *Applications in human resources,* p. 296. Mason, OH: Cengage Learning.
11. Carson, M. (2006). Saying it like it isn't: The pros and cons of 360-degree feedback. *Business Horizons, 49,* 395-402, p. 395

SECTION V:

MARKETING SYSTEMS

Marketing is the function that supports exchanges between a customer and a business. Externally, it helps camp administrators

- examine outside environmental factors that influence a summer sports camp,
- analyze consumers' behavior and their decision-making process, and
- evaluate the overall market of sports education and the segmentation of that market. In addition, segmentation will identify niche opportunities and a defined target market on which a camp can focus its efforts.

Internally, sports camp marketing

- examines product and service selection and development,
- provides foundations for pricing a camp's products and services,
- clarifies the choices of distribution of a camp's products and services, and
- communicates the benefits to potential consumers of the camp's products and services.

The application of marketing by a camp administrator will increase the camp's exposure as well as the camp's revenues. It creates desire and action in the camp's customers and, if used correctly, it can take an operation to another level and competitive position.

Marketing communication contains six primary promotional elements: advertising, direct marketing, sales promotion, personal selling, public relations, and technology. The promotional mix of these tools is accomplished through a planned process that takes into account goals, budgets, and, ultimately, the camp's target market. The successful combination of these tools can maximize a summer sports camp's exposure, image, and customer base. However, it should be restated that marketing communication is a part of the whole marketing effort. By itself and without the proper background concepts of the marketing mix, marketing communication will inevitably fail to achieve its goals.

10

Marketing Foundations

INTRODUCTION

Marketing interacts with almost all of the camp's functions. Even beyond that, marketing can control a majority of the camp's components. The term marketing is probably one of the most misused and misunderstood words in today's business world. The first thing that one associates with marketing is advertising. The function of advertising is just one aspect of the total concept of marketing. Marketing is also involved with product selection, customer research, distribution of the product, pricing decisions, and numerous other administrative elements.

Marketing Defined

The American Marketing Association defines marketing as "the activity, set of institutions, and processes for creating, communicating, delivering, and exchanging offerings that have value for customers, clients, partners, and society at large."[1]

The goal of this section is to examine the primary elements of marketing as they relate to camp administration.

© Krisdog | Dreamstime.com

Importance of Marketing for Sports Camps

The significance of the marketing function for camps cannot be stressed enough. Marketing produces customer value, satisfaction, and relationship development through the model of *utility*. "Utility is the value or expected value associated with an item. A product has utility either directly or indirectly. . . . [S]ervices also have utility. . . . [P]eople exchange money, in part, for the utility present in the goods and services they purchase."[2]

Camp Tip

The American Marketing Association is a tremendous resource for marketing information and educational options.

In addition to utility, marketing systems present the organization with elements such as information on the summer sports camp's external environment, which can facilitate long- and short-term decisions; details on the make-up of the camp's customer base, which can concentrate resources; details on the make-up of the camp's competitors, which is an essential component of survival; and a logical process for the development of new products, pricing options, where to place products and services, and promotional considerations.

MARKETING RESEARCH FOR SPORTS CAMPS

In most camp settings, because of time limitations, marketing research is restricted despite being of great consequence for decision making. Operating under this idea, marketing research must be as focused as possible to maximize the decreased time available. The question then becomes, "How can a camp administrator solve the challenge of obtaining critical information to support decision making while knowing that marketing research is probably beyond his or her time availability, typical life experience, and education?" The answer relates to secondary data research.

> Secondary data refer to data that were collected earlier but are still related to the research question. This data may come from within the sport organization or from outside the organization. . . . [I]t is sometimes impossible to find data relevant to the problem at hand. In that case, research must turn to other data collection alternative, primary data. Primary data is information gathered for the specific research question at hand.[3]

In other words, primary research is conducted by the camp for a specific need or problem. Secondary research is conducted by someone else to solve similar needs or problems.

Secondary research has advantages and disadvantages in relation to primary research. Once again, the advantages are mostly in expense and time. Secondary research just needs to be uncovered rather than conducted. In some cases, the time and cash savings are enormous. The disadvantages of secondary research include three elements:

1. **Problem to fit:** Does the secondary research fit the camp's special needs or problems?

2. **Outdated information:** Since the research was done in the past, how obsolete has it become?

3. **Confidence in research:** Was the research completed by reliable researchers who were objective and unbiased?

If the camp administrator can answer that the secondary research fits the camp's situation, is timely, and was prepared by a trustworthy source, then secondary data is tremendously valuable. The following is a list of possible avenues to pursue secondary data:

- Libraries, public and academic
- E-Libraries and commercial sources
- Periodicals such as journals and magazines
- Electronic sources such as the Internet and search engines
- United States governmental sources
- Directories and trade association publications

The two areas on which most camps should concentrate their marketing research efforts are (1) competition and (2) potential customers. Competitive research should center on, but not be limited to, the following questions:

- Who is our competition—both direct (other summer sports camps) and indirect (such as general recreation camps)?
- What is the size and history of our competitors' camp operations?
- What are the competitive strategies of our competitors?
- What does our competition's SWOT analysis look like? Does it give them a practical advantage?
- What is the structure of their camps?
- Where do their camps operate? What are the advantages associated with these locales?
- What is the model of the competitor's instructional sessions?
- What are the competitions' principal goals for running a camp?
- Who is their target market? What is the target market's opinion of the competitors' camps?
- Do the competitors have strategic alliances?

    When researching customers for a camp, the following questions are among those that need to be investigated:
- From the camps being offered, what is the target market's customer profile like? What is the target market's flexible/discretionary income?
- How great is the overall potential market for the camp in the operational area?
- Who are the participants? Who is the decision maker who will purchase/pay for the camp?

- What are the driving forces behind the participants' motives to attend a camp?

- What association does the participant have with the sport and its governing body?

- Are there customer groups, like teams, clubs, and educational institutions, that should be targeted?

The more information about a camp's competition and customer base, the better the marketing decisions for the camp. A complete customer profile is helpful when framing marketing and promotional strategies. Make sure that the four major components are described in the profile (to be discussed in the next section): demographics (characteristics), psychographics (lifestyles), behaviors (tangible actions), and geographic (locations).

MARKET SEGMENTATION AND TARGET MARKETING

A market is "a group of potential customers with similar needs who are willing to exchange something of value with sellers offering various goods and services—that is, ways of satisfying those needs."[4] A target market is merely a group of people inside a market with even more clear characteristics on which a camp can focus its marketing effort. For example, the consumer market for a sports camp is in the education industry. One can then break down the broad market classification of education into the more detailed, but still sizeable, category of sports education. From there, divide the sports education market into the specific target market of sports education customers for a specific sport, in a particular geographic area, with a distinct income level, etc. The more clear-cut the camp's target market, the more reasoned the camp's marketing efforts.

The potential ways to break a camp market into distinct segments are presented in Table 10.1.

Demographics are associated with population characteristics; geographic criteria relate to locations; psychographics are lifestyle choices; behavioral features are an individual and/or group use of the product or service. To get an accurate market segmentation, each category and subcategory must be examined for its relevance to the summer sports camp market. By questioning a market's demographics, geographics, and purchasing behavior, one is developing segmentation profiles of individuals and groups.

Table 10.1. Segmentation Factors

Geographic Features
global location/country, financial level of geographic area, urban/rural, population concentration, geographic environmental elements (temperature, terrain, etc.)

Demographic Features
male/female, maturity level/age, earning potential, household factors (spouse, children, relatives, etc.), profession, educational degree, religious convictions, ethnic group, social status

Psychographic Features
standard of living, activities, qualities, interests

Behavioristic Features
patterns of consumption, previous purchases, loyalty to a product/service, consumer preference

---

The most useful application of Table 10.1 is for identifying the camp's specific target market. With one's particular sport in mind, go through each category and develop a specific profile of the target market group. Ask the following questions:

1. Who are they? Go through the demographic and psychographics subcategories.

2. Where are they? Go through the geographic subcategories.

3. When will they buy? How will they buy? Why will they buy? Go through the behavioral subcategories.

A few important points on identifying target market segments:

- Sports camp, at each level of ability, will have its own unique segment(s) or niche(s).

- Is it feasible to have more than one target market segment for a summer sports camp? Absolutely. One might come up with several target market segments in which the groups described are ideal for one's sport and camp.

In selecting the target market(s), a camp administrator should consider the following points:

- **Measurable.** Can you quantify the segment?

- **Accessible.** Do you have access to the market?

- **Substantial.** Is the segment of sufficient size to warrant attention as a segment? Further, is the segment declining, maturing, or growing?

- **Profitable.** Does concentrating on the segment provide sufficient profitability to make it worthwhile?

- **Compatible with competition.** To what extent do your major competitors have an interest in the segment? Is it an active interest or of negligible concern to you competition?

- **Effective.** Does your organization have sufficient skills and resources to serve the segment effectively?

- **Defendable.** Does your firm have the capability to defend itself against the attack of a major competitor?[5]

Once again, segment size and growth relate to sales, growth rate, and profitability of a segment. Segment attractiveness defines the strength of the competition's ability to go after a given market segment. The ability of customers to switch to another camp affects a segment's attractiveness, so the availability of other camps needs to be taken into account. The stronger each of these alternatives is, the less attractive the segment. A camp's objectives and resources must always form the backdrop to determine if the segment is in line with the camp's goals and whether the camp possesses the capabilities, assets, and funding needed to take advantage of that segment.

If one can verify that the segment being evaluated is in an attractive group that presents an opportunity, has good profitability and growth potential, and is in line with the camp's mission and resources, then it is an excellent segment to pursue.

Camp Tip

When determining which target markets are appropriate for the camp, do not dismiss any potential groups solely on the basis of opinion. Get concrete information. It is very possible that some of the camp's most enthusiastic customers could be from profile groups that, on the surface, one would reject.

Camp Tip

In selecting target markets, know the camp's resource limitations. For small camps, a focused, niche strategy can present a strong competitive advantage. If the target market niche is successfully captured by the camp first, the camp will be identified with that niche and be on the ground floor of future increased growth. The key is finding a niche group that can sustain the camp currently and also shows long-term growth potential.

EXCHANGES

Exchanges can best be defined by the following:

> Marketing occurs when people decide to satisfy needs and wants through exchanges. Exchange is the act of obtaining a desired object from someone by offering something in return . . . [and] is the core concept of the discipline of marketing. For a voluntary exchange to take place, five conditions must be satisfied:
>
> 1. There are at least two parties.
> 2. Each party has something that may be of value to the other party.
> 3. Each party is capable of communication and delivery.
> 4. Each party is free to accept or reject the other party's offer.
> 5. Each party believes it is appropriate or desirable to deal with the other party.[6]

The model of exchanges is at the heart of all business actions. Exchanges deal with benefits. In other words, does the consumer experience a positive benefit—material, social, personal, or sensory—and did that exchange provide a value-for-value trade? If so, the consumer will seek out that exchange again. If not, then the service or product in need will be purchased elsewhere. The job of a camp administrator is to provide the most value to their customers so they will develop a strong need that, in turn, will promote future exchanges.

APPENDIX 10.1: CONSUMER DECISION PROCESS

Identifying how the consumer makes purchase choices is crucial to understanding how to develop and retain camp customers. A substantial portion of practically every marketing text published today is dedicated to the fundamental consumer decision process. The five-step process is as follows:

Step 1: Problem recognition

Step 2: Information search

Step 3: Alternative evaluation

Step 4: Purchase decision

Step 5: Post-purchase evaluation[7]

Every single purchase made by a consumer, no matter how large or small, goes through this five-step process. Sometimes the process can happen in a split second and in other cases, it can take hours, days, or longer.

Step 1: Problem Recognition

We all have needs. They are the elements that provide each of us with the tools to survive, socialize, and achieve esteem. In 1954, Abraham Maslow, in his historic, groundbreaking book *Motivation and Personality,* contends that needs are ranked and the only way to attain higher, more luxurious desires is to make sure that our critical physiological and safety needs are satisfied first. Figure 10.1 is his graphic picture of the hierarchy of needs (in ascending form).

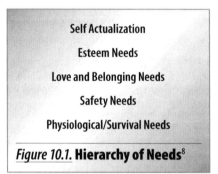

Self Actualization

Esteem Needs

Love and Belonging Needs

Safety Needs

Physiological/Survival Needs

Figure 10.1. **Hierarchy of Needs**[8]

Understanding human needs is the basis for identifying the camp's target market, as well as what customers in that target market are looking for in the camp's product or service. For example, an individual who is looking to satisfy the bottom level of needs in Maslow's hierarchy model (physiological and safety) would not be concerned, at that point in time, with attending a camp. For target market identification, sports education focuses on groups who want to fulfill higher needs of belonging, esteem, and self-actualization. In the most direct terms, our product of sports education is vying to meet the needs of people with flexible and discretionary income over and above their survival and safety needs. The practical application of this theory narrows the market substantially.

Step 2: Information Search

Once people recognize a need that they must or would like to satisfy, they proceed to gather information about it. The information search

> may be internal, retrieving knowledge from memory or perhaps genetic tendencies, or it may be external, collecting information from peers, family, and the marketplace. Sometimes consumers search passively by simply becoming more receptive to information around them, whereas at other times they engage in active search behavior, such as researching consumer publications, paying attention to ads, searching the Internet, or venturing to shopping malls and other retail outlets…The length and depth of search is determined by variables such as personality, social class, income, size of purchase, past experiences, prior brand perceptions, and customer satisfaction. If customers are delighted with the brand of product they currently use, they may repurchase the brand with little if any search behavior, making it more difficult for competitive products to catch their attention. That's why

victorious firms place high priority on keeping customers satisfied. When customers are unhappy with current products or brands, search expands to include other alternatives.[9]

The category of product or service will typically determine the extent to which individuals will seek out information for it. Products and services are typically classified as follows:

- **Convenience products/services:** Little time and mental effort put into information search, low cost relative to customer base, everyday common purchases, and low switching costs.

- **Shopping products/services:** Moderate amount of time and mental effort exerted for information searching, substantial (but not major) cost, and infrequent purchases.

- **Specialty products/services:** Vast amount of information search, big ticket and high-cost purchases for customer base, rare purchases.

Sports education services need to be understood in terms of the type of product (convenience, shopping, or specialty) they represent to the customers. Each camp has to identify its product classification, as this will guide the marketing efforts and determine how much information the customer will demand.

Step 3: Alternative Evaluation

This is the point in the process when consumers, after gathering all the significant information needed, look at all of their choices. In other words, consumers compare the possible options that might satisfy their needs.

Decision making involves determining the value or adequacy of the alternatives that were generated. In other words, which solution would be the best. . . . Fundamental to this process is to predict the consequences that will occur if the various options are put into effect.[10]

Consumer factors that can stimulate actions include:

- *personal background factors,* such as education, family influences, childhood experiences, income level, peer groups, social status, etc.;

- *geographical factors,* such as rural versus urban, metropolis versus small town, north versus south, etc.;

© Bradcalkins | Dreamstime.com

- *knowledge factors,* such as exposure to literature and media influences, past usage (directly or through others' experiences), sampling, etc.; and

- *attitude and motivational elements,* such as feelings and opinions, evaluation processes, psychographics/lifestyles, etc.

Camp Tip

A camp administrator's job is to convey as much quality information as possible to current and potential campers. The key is to find out the best and easiest avenues to convey the camp information. This is done by understanding what information the campers will use and then arranging information to fit their needs.

These factors are what the camp's advertising and promotional campaigns should target. The desire is to have customers perceive that the camp's product (athletic education) is the finest option to fulfill their needs.

Step 4: Purchase Decision

At some point in the buying process, the consumer must stop searching for and evaluating information about alternative brands in the evoke set and make a purchase decision. As an outcome of the alternative evaluation stage, the consumer may develop a purchase intention or predisposition to buy a certain brand. Purchase intentions are generally based on a matching of purchase motives with attributes or characteristics of brands under consideration.[11]

From a sports camp standpoint, one simple idea is associated with the action of purchasing: Make it as easy and painless as possible. The worst thing that a camp administrator can do is to make the purchase experience for the potential camper complex and confusing.

Step 5: Post Purchase Evaluation

The final step in the decision-making process relates to the camper's satisfaction with the service purchased, as this will influence how he or she will choose and behave the next time the same need surfaces. There is one phenomenon that takes place in this stage on which a camp administrator must concentrate and attach importance: *cognitive dissonance* or *buyer remorse.* Cognitive dissonance occurs

in situations where there is high involvement, a socially visible purchasing experience, or if the product or service is expensive . . . consumers often experience doubt after purchases . . . because of the investment in time, money, and ego, it is natural for a consumer to question a decision.[12]

An outstanding way to minimize buyer remorse is to provide the camper with a quality service (quality sports education experience). The more costly the service, the more one needs to concentrate on cognitive dissonance. Followup contacts, personal notes, special promotions, and other related perks are all ways to ease buyer remorse.

ENDNOTES

1. The American Marketing Association Releases New Definition for Marketing. (2008). *American Marketing Association News Release.*
2. Clow, K. E., & Baack, D. (2002). *Integrated advertising, promotion, and marketing communication,* p. 170. Upper Saddle River, NJ: Prentice Hall.
3. Shank, M. D. (2005). *Sports marketing: A strategic perspective* (3rd edition), p. 105. Upper Saddle River, NJ: Prentice Hall.

4. Perreault, W. D., Cannon, J. P., & McCarthy, E. J. (2010). *Essentials of marketing: A marketing strategy planning approach* (12th edition), p. 685. New York, NY: McGraw-Hill/Irwin.

5. Paley, N. (2000). *How to develop a strategic marketing plan: A step-by-step guide,* p. 163. Boca Raton, FL: St. Lucie Press.

6. Kotler, P. (2003). *Marketing management* (11th edition), p. 12. Upper Saddle River, NJ: Prentice Hall.

7. Belch, G. E., & Belch, M. A. (2009). *Advertising and promotion: An integrated marketing communication perspective* (8th edition), p. 113. Boston, MA: McGraw Hill/Irwin.

8. Maslow, A. (1954). *Motivation and personality.* New York, NY: Harper and Row.

9. Blackwell, R. D., Miniard, P. W., & Engel, J. F. (2001). *Consumer behavior* (9th edition), pp. 73-74. Orlando, FL: Harcourt College Publishers.

10. Bateman, T. S., & Snell, S. A. (2011). *Management: Leading and collaborating in a competitive world* (9th edition), p. 91. New York, NY: McGraw-Hill/Irwin.

11. Shank, M. D. (2005). *Sports marketing: A strategic perspective* (3rd edition), p. 127. Upper Saddle River, NJ: Prentice Hall.

12. Clow, K. E., & Baack, D. (2002). *Integrated advertising, promotion, and marketing communication,* p. 163. Upper Saddle River, NJ: Prentice Hall.

Marketing Mix

MARKETING MIX

A key concept in marketing a camp is the *marketing mix*. The marketing mix, also known as the *4 Ps of marketing*, details how the camp administrator will create, price, distribute, and promote the product that the camp produces.

4 Ps of Marketing

In the business world, the marketing mix is defined as

> the proper blending of the basic elements of product, price, promotion and place into an integrated marketing program. . . . [T]he right product for the target market must be developed. Place refers to the channels of distribution. Promotion refers to any method that communicates to the target market. The right price should be set to attract customers and make a profit.[1]

Kotler (2003) analyzes the 4 Ps in further detail. Figure 11.1 is an overview of his concepts.[2]

All four of these marketing elements play a role in a camp, and promotion will be detailed exclusively in Chapter 12. However, camps produce services that have educational value rather than actual physical presence. "Services have four unique characteristics that distinguish them from goods: intangibility, inseparability, heterogeneity, and perishability."[3]

Marketing Mix	
PRODUCT	**PRICE**
Product Variety	List Price
Design	Discounts
Quality	Allowances
Features	Payments
Brand Name	Credit Terms
Packaging	
Sizes	
Services	
Warranties	
Returns	
Target Market	
PLACE	**PROMOTION**
Channels	Sales Promos
Coverage	Advertising
Assortment	Sales Force
Locations	Public Relations
Inventory	Direct Marketing

Figure 11.1. **The 4 Ps of Marketing**[4]

As stated earlier, camps are in the education market. A camp is a set of services that are consumed via camper participation and direct involvement. The *inseparability* of a service refers to the idea that the consumer is using a service at the same time as he or she pays for it. In other words, the camper is present during the delivery of the camp instruction. While products can be very similar (if not precisely alike), services such as camps are unique. Finally, services such as camps are perishable because they are time specific. Once an educational session is over, a camper can never see it again in present time. With this difference between services and products, we can adapt the marketing mix concept to camp services.

Product/Service/Output

As a camp administrator, one's primary concern should be with the camp's product or service. The unconditional focus should be on quality and value. Quality can relate to the camp's performance, presentation, facilities, administration, and any other aspects that directly or indirectly influence its output. Without quality, marketing and promotions break down.

Another product/service issue relates to the *uniqueness* of one's camp operation. Uniqueness is used to separate the camp from its competition and to build the image—also known as branding—of the sports camp in the minds of customers and supporters.

A further major marketing product/service consideration that affects camps is the selection of the type of educational services/sessions the camp is currently offering, and the educational services/camp sessions it is going to highlight in the future. Some camps may be, at a given point in time, restricted to emphasizing base sport educational services. Lack of resources, poor administration, and a lack of personnel are a few of the reasons to contemplate a single-service marketing strategy. However, in most cases, camps have capabilities to mature beyond the base educational services. Expanding the camp's services into different levels of instruction, merchandising, and new camp endeavors (specialty camps, coaches' clinics, team camps, etc.) are just some of the ways to diversify.

The following areas and questions need to be addressed when developing the camp's products and services:

- Customers do not purchase a product or service: They purchase the benefits that come from a product or service. What benefits will the camp provide the athlete participants? Can those benefits be communicated in a convincing, clear message?

- Product quality cannot be sacrificed. Besides the loss of current and future participants, there are safety issues that require quality. How will the camp realize and surpass quality expectations? How will the camp administrator determine and quantify the intangible service quality offered by the camp? What systems will be in place to guarantee quality control?

- Sports camps are a service and differ from tangible products in that they are
  - more people oriented,
  - perishable and consumed at the point of delivery,
  - intangible and such that mistakes are harder to correct, and
  - unique from session to session.

- How will the camp ensure consistency and superior instruction in its services? How can the camp maximize these distinct service elements to provide the best possible experience for participants?

- Not all opportunities are always right for all organizations. What type of product line—camp instructional sessions, for instance—should the camp offer to its present and future participants? Are these opportunities (camp sessions) right for the operation?

- The ultimate goal of a camp's service is brand name recognition. How can a camp develop its brand recognition? What product/service elements should be emphasized that will lead to strong branding?

- Continuous improvement is an important ingredient to fight complacency. How can camps enhance their already recognized product? Are these improvements sound? Does the camp have the resources to initiate these improvements?

Camp Tip

When attempting to form new camp services, at all costs avoid gimmicks and publicity stunts that will damage the integrity of the current summer sports camp. While these marketing techniques will direct short-term attention to the camp, their long-term effects could be lasting, even irreparable. Uniqueness with a high-class reputation will bring extended growth.

Pricing

Now that there is a desired service (whether a recognized, conventional summer sports camp or a new and innovative camp), one will need to price it for profitability while still maintaining and increasing the camp's customer base. Pricing decisions

> influence everything from its marketing and sales efforts to its operation and strategy. Price is the monetary value of a product or service in the marketplace; it is a measurement of what the customer must give up to obtain various goods and services. Price is also a signal of a product's or service's value to an individual, and different customers assign different values to the same goods and services. . . . [P]rice must be compatible with the customers' perception of value.[4]

By understanding the basic concepts of pricing, camp administrators can be more conscious, in general, of pricing decisions and how they can affect the overall camp. The following are a few relevant points when discussing camp pricing.

1. Pricing for a new sports camp must be in harmony with its overall operational strategy (low cost, differentiations, best value, or niche). For example, if a low-cost strategy is employed, prices charged to participants and the subsequent profit margins are typically smaller than those of competitors that employ a differentiation or best-value strategy. With the current overall pricing strategy, can the camp meet its financial responsibilities? With prices established by the strategic camp plan, what would be the breakeven point (in number of participants) to cover both fixed and variable costs?

2. External environmental factors can have a major impact on pricing decisions. The primary external factor that can affect pricing is the economy and purchasing power. How can economic conditions sway camp pricing decisions? Is the camp's target market drastically affected by economic downturns? What pricing tactics can the camp employ to combat a sluggish economy? How will the camp be shaped by these elements? Will the camp need to restrategize its pricing to account for these factors?

3. *Price elasticity* is the concept of price changes and their effect on demand. Specifically, price elasticity reveals how sensitive the change in demand for a service is when there is a change in price for that service. If the camp's pricing is elastic, adjustments in price produce radical swings in the number of people who want it. Conversely, if a change in the camp's price has little or no impact on the demand, then that situation is known as *inelastic pricing*. There is also a situation known as *unitary demand*. This is when a percentage change in price furnishes an exact percentage change in demand. The questions that

need to be answered: How much price elasticity does the camp have? At what point will the camp price itself out of the market? What has been the price elasticity history of the operation? Under which situation can the camp maximize profits (highest price with estimated demand)?

4. Once a camp administrator has a picture of the price elasticity of the camp's services, the pricing goals for those services need to be generated. One should price the camp's services to keep them in harmony with the camp's overall goals. These objectives should be straightforward and easily understandable. An objective fixed on survival is essentially an emergency approach to pricing that is designed to keep the camp afloat. In these cases the only consideration is to situate the price at whatever level makes it possible just to keep the camp going. Pricing for a fixed return is principally done by establishing a desired profit over and above the estimated costs and working the price to achieve the projected amount. Strengthening or enlarging market share and maintaining competitive position bases the price not only on what the competition is doing, but on how one can aggressively establish and acquire more customers.

5. To establish a price point for a camp, three factors must be considered: cost, competition, and value. From a cost viewpoint, prices must be established to cover expenditures associated with each camper as well as the camp's overall fixed operating expenses. A camp administrator must construct a breakeven analysis—a breakdown of costs associated with projected revenue—to know when the camp's expenses are covered at a certain price level. The second factor to research relates to the market and a comparison of competitors' prices. Clearly stated, how competitors price their similar camps will directly affect the foundation of how the camp prices out its products and services. The final component of pricing deals with the value customers put on the camp's services. The more value, and subsequent demand, the customer places on the camp, the more control a camp administrator has over the price of those services. It should be stated that each of these can be used separately to devise a camp's price structure. However, a blending of all three methods (cost, competition, and value) will give a more precise and realistic picture of the camp's price structure.

6. The concept of price skimming versus price penetration parallels the pricing philosophy of new offerings in summer sports camp. *Price skimming* is the introduction of a new service into the market with a high price. The reason for choosing this type of pricing strategy is to recapture as much initial cost as possible with limited sales. *Price penetration* is the introduction of a new service at a minimal cost to

gain as many new customers as possible. The major purpose for this type of pricing approach is to get as much of the overall market share as immediately as possible.

7. Pricing a camp's services can have a psychological influence on current and prospective customers. A product or service with a high price can convey superior quality (whether that quality exists or not). This type of psychological pricing is known as *prestige pricing*. Conversely, a low product price could communicate a lack of quality (again, whether quality exists or not). Another psychological pricing technique is *odd-even pricing*. Odd-even pricing is when a price is established that makes a customer think that the price is lower than it really is. For example, $19.99 is essentially $20.00, while customers will often acknowledge the price as $19.00. *Bundle pricing* can also be a psychological pricing tactic. By combining a set of camp services, a camp administrator can increase sales of multiple items, increase offerings, and have a better overall package price for the customer.

8. Discounting is used when a camp wants to stimulate sales in a specific timeframe. In other words, discounting is a short-term solution that can only be applied for limited periods. If it is discovered that the price level established is elastic at a certain level, a reconsideration of the camp's price rather than repeated discounting should be examined. Other price discounts can encompass:

   - *Quantity discounts:* Provide customers with discounts related to the amount they purchase.
   - *Seasonal discounts:* Used to balance out seasonal fluctuation in sales.
   - *Early payment discounts:* Used to encourage faster payments, decreases in accounts receivables, and increases in cash flow.
   - *Special-event discounts:* Used to promote a camp's special event and increase awareness.
   - *Repeat business discounts:* Special discounts provided to repeat customers.

9. Other discussion points related to pricing a camp include the following:

   - If the camp is pricing to capture market share from its competition, could that create a price war? If so, how well can the camp handle price competition?
   - How similar is the market price of related camps to the camp's pricing strategy?
   - How will camp prices be determined for all of the instructional sessions—standardized hourly pricing or by value given?

Camp Tip

Remember that discounting is a short-term solution to stimulate sales and support. Abuse of this strategy can devalue the overall worth and distinctiveness of a summer sports camp.

Place/Distribution

The basic difference between a tangible good and an intangible service (like sports camp instruction) is most obvious when discussing distribution. There are two ways to dispense camp services: Either the customers come to the camp's location, or one must take the camp's service to them. The key to making a good choice between these two is accessibility. Ask which approach has the greatest potential to get the camp the largest number of customers. For example, if one's camp is exceptionally visible, is in a heavily populated area, and is easily accessible, the camp's service distribution would be to have the customers come to the camp's facilities. However, if the camp's operational home is in a remote location with poor exposure, creative distribution might be required. The camp administrator may need to take the camp's services on the road to maximize customer interaction and sales.

Location and facility determinations are related directly to the third marketing mix element, place (or service distribution). Open discussions with camp personnel should relate to the accessibility of the facility for camp participants; dimensions, capacity, and appropriateness of the building(s) for the projected operations; condition of the facility (e.g., in disrepair or poor condition?); safety of structure as well as safety of the general location; and overall customer impressions of facility and locality.

Other questions relating to the summer sports camp's location and facility that can be discussed could include

- Can the existing facility be modified and used for the camp?
- Will the facility be vacant for the camp's projected dates and times (in-house or outsourced)?
- Will housing be necessary and, if so, will it be on campus or outsourced to private establishments (hotels, motels, other educational institutions)?
- Is parking and traffic flow a consideration for the camp?
- Are there medical/training facilities at the location? If so, are they accessible to camp participants?
- If conditioning sessions (aerobic, plyometric, weight, etc.) are an ingredient of the instruction, does the facility have the capability to conduct these sessions?
- Does the facility have secure storage areas for equipment and camp merchandise?
- Are there locker rooms on hand and are they suitable for camp operations?
- If camp instruction sessions are open to the public (parents, college recruiters, etc.), is there proper seating available that does not disrupt camp operations?

© Lunamarina | Dreamstime.com

- Does the facility have good quality ventilation and air conditioning?
- Does the facility have an isolated staff area that can be designated for meetings, hospitality, and relaxation between sessions?

The better each of these facility and location items, the more a camp's service will be perceived as having exceptional quality. Additionally, better facilities can influence pricing and assist with promotional communication messages.

ENDNOTES

1. Megginson, L. C., Byrd, M. J., & Megginson, W. L. (2006). *Small business management: An entrepreneur's guidebook,* p. 187. New York, NY: McGraw-Hill/Irwin.
2. Kotler, P. (2003). *Marketing management* (11th edition), p. 16. Upper Saddle River, NJ: Prentice Hall.
3. Lamb, C. W., Hair, J. F., & McDaniel, C. (2003). *Essentials of marketing* (3rd edition), p. 267. Mason, OH: Thompson South-Western.
4. Scarborough, N. M. (2011). *Essentials of entrepreneurship and small business management* (6th edition), p. 301. Upper Saddle River, NJ: Pearson Prentice Hall.

12

Promotion

PROMOTION

Promotion is the fourth and final component of the marketing mix. Promotion is

communicating information between sellers and potential buyers to influence attitudes and behaviors. . . . The main promotional job is to tell targeted customers that the right product is available, at the right price, at the right place. . . . What the marketer communicates is determined by customer needs and attitudes. . . . How the message is delivered depends on what blend of various promotional methods the marketing communicator chooses.[1]

© WVU courtesy of WVU Photo Services

Camp Tip

Positive word of mouth is the ultimate aim of any marketing communication. If one can get the camp's supporters talking about the camp's products and services in an optimistic—maybe even enthusiastic—fashion, they will generate a snowball effect that can take the camp beyond all expectations. A critical advantage of positive word of mouth is that one will need to spend fewer resources on marketing communication in the future.

Promotional Tools

Promotion is, in fact, marketing communication. Marketing communication consists of five traditional promotional tools and a new and evolving sixth tool: technology. Marilyn Stone and John Desmond describe the traditional promotional tools as follows:

Advertising. Advertising refers to a paid form of non-personal communication about an organization and its products that is transmitted to a target population through a mass medium. Traditional mass media include television, newspapers, radio, posters, transport and outdoor displays.

Direct marketing. Direct marketing has evolved out of the direct mail industry and incorporates telephone selling and email. Often, direct marketing is used as a pre-sell technique prior to a sales call, to generate orders and to follow up a sale. Direct marketing requires good database management techniques, as errors can create bad feelings.

Sales promotion. Sales promotion offers some form of incentive to purchase a product. Marketers devise sales promotions to produce immediate sales increases.

Personal selling. Personal selling is the process of informing customers and persuading them to purchase products through personal communication.

Publicity. Publicity refers to the link between marketing and public relations.[2]

The newest promotional tool that is showing tremendous potential is promotional technology. These virtual instruments consist primarily of web-based promotions, electronic communication, and social media.

Marketing Communication Budgeting

Budgeting is the control function that assists a camp administrator in establishing and maintaining guidelines for spending. When constructed correctly, these tools help forecast needs and describe circumstances through solid numbers. However, budgeting money for marketing communications and promotion is as much a philosophical issue as it is financial. In other words, one's way of thinking about designating money to the function of marketing communication will often influence the extent to which it is financed. Some camp administrators possess the attitude that marketing communication is a luxury and whatever is available at the end of the financing/budgeting process is what gets assigned to marketing communication. More progressive administrators are realizing the worth of marketing communication and have prioritized its budgeting and financing.

Specific techniques associated with the nuts and bolts of marketing communication budgeting can include the following methods:

> **Arbitrary allocation:** The simplest, yet most unsystematic, approach to determining promotional budgeting is called arbitrary allocation. Using this method, sports marketers set the budget in isolation of other critical factors. . . . [P]romotional budgets are established after the organization's other costs are considered.

Competitive parity: Setting promotional budgets based on what competitors are spending (competitive parity) is often used for certain product categories in sports marketing.

Percentage of sales: The percentage of sales method of promotional budget allocation is based on determining some standard percentage of promotional spending and applying this proportion to either past or forecasted sales to arrive at the amount to be spent. . . . It has a number of shortcomings. . . . With sales declining, it may be more appropriate to increase (rather than decrease) promotional spending. A second major shortcoming of using this method is the notion that budgeting is very loosely, if at all, tied to the promotional objective.

Objective and task method: Objective and task method could be characterized as the most logical and systematic. The objective and task method identifies the promotional objectives, defines the communication tools and tasks needed to meet those objectives, and then adds up the cost of the planned activities.[3]

One final point on marketing communication budgeting: There are clear dangers in underfunding a camp's marketing communication and promotional activities. Underfunding restricts the success of communication tactics and limits a camp's projected exposure. Conversely, overfunding marketing communication tactics is just as damaging. Precious resources will be wasted and other strategies the camp might want to pursue will be missed due to the lack of funds. The key to a good marketing communication budget is knowing the funds needed to accomplish communication goals and spending the exact amount to achieve those objectives.

Marketing Communication Goals

Prior to discussing these six promotional and communication tools, a camp administrator will need to briefly examine goals pertaining to marketing communication:

- **Build awareness:** New products and new companies are often unknown to a market, which means initial promotional efforts must focus on establishing an identity. In this situation the marketer must focus promotion to: effectively reach customers and tell the market who they are and what they have to offer.

- **Create interest:** Moving a customer from awareness of a product to making a purchase can present a significant challenge. . . . The focus on creating messages that convince customers that a need exists has been the hallmark of marketing for a long time with promotional appeals targeted at a basic human characteristic such as emotions, fears, sex, and humor.

- **Provide information:** Some promotion is designed to assist customers in the search stage of the purchasing process. In some cases, such as when a product is so novel it creates a new category or product and has few competitors, the information is simply intended to explain what the product is and may not mention any competitors. In other situations, where the product competes in an existing market, informational promotion may be used to help with a product positioning strategy and creating primary demand.

- **Stimulate demand:** The right promotion can drive customers to make a purchase.
- **Reinforce the brand:** Once a purchase is made, a marketer can use promotion to help build a strong relationship that can lead to the purchaser becoming a loyal customer.[4]

As a camp administrator, map out the camp's goals for promotions. Can one undertake and achieve multiple promotional goals? Absolutely. In other words, can a camp administrator put together a promotional communication strategy by using advertising, direct marketing, sales promotions, public relations, personal selling, and technology or a combination of these that not only generates a buzz for the camp but also retains and even increases the camp's customer bases? Yes. It is more difficult to have multiple goals, but if one is inventive and can think the campaign through, there are no limits.

After forming and defining the goals for the camp's promotion, examine the communication tools of advertising, direct marketing, sales promotion, public relations/ publicity, personal selling, and technology. It should be noted that a close examination of each of these tools is well beyond the scope of this book. In fact, each of these areas is a specialized career. Thus, it is not the purpose of this text to enable each reader to become an authority on these tools and their use, but rather to assist the reader in gaining a working knowledge that will allow each of these tools to be successfully adapted and used.

Advertising

The first promotional communication tool at a camp administrator's disposal is advertising. Advertising is

a non-personal sales presentation communicated through media or non-media forms to influence a large number of consumers. . . . [I]t is a common method for promoting products and services. Although advertising is generally more expensive than other methods, it can reach many consumers. . . . Brand advertising is a non-personal sales presentation about a specific brand. . . . Comparative advertising is intended to persuade customers to purchase a specific product by demonstrating a brand's superiority by comparison with other competing brands. . . . . Reminder advertising is intended to remind consumers of a product's existence. . . . Institutional advertising is a non-personal sales presentation about a specific institution. . . . Industry advertising is a non-personal presentation about a specific industry.[5]

Advertising Avenues/Media Mix

The media mix is the "combination of advertising media used in pursuing the promotional objectives of a marketing plan. Considering more than one media type can optimize a plan's effectiveness and take advantage of the unique advantages of each type."[6] The types of media are detailed in Table 12.1.

From this list, a camp administrator can begin to uncover which advertising communication tool is necessary based on the target market. In the 2003 text *Principles of Marketing*, Charles Lamb, Joe Hair, and Carl McDaniel explain the advantages and disadvantages of each type of advertising/media communication tool. Table 12.2 is a summary of their ideas.[7]

After researching each type of advertising communication tool for its relevant advantages and disadvantages, the most important criteria for selecting an advertising mix, a package of advertising tools that will promote the camp, is financial. The advertising goal from a financial standpoint is simple. Which advertising tool or tools should the camp use to strengthen its target market exposure and get the most from its limited advertising dollars? This is where the previously discussed subject of segmentation and targeting comes into play and affects advertising communication. Knowing your current and prospective customers is key. Through market segmentation and target market selection, a camp administrator can get a well-defined profile of current and potential customers. This segment profile will furnish answers to questions such as the following:

- Who are they?
- Where are they?
- What type of people are they?
- What are their demographics? Psychographics? Geographic? Lifestyles?
- When is the best time to communicate with them?
- How often do they need promotional communication?

© Tmcnem | Dreamstime.com

Camp Tip

The key to any paid advertising is reaching and then impacting the target market. Within budget limits, ask which advertising tools will have the most influence on the projected audience. Typically, quantity of messages communicated is not as important as quality of messages communicated. Think about which advertising tools will provide the summer sports camp with the highest-quality, most powerful message that will reach the target market efficiently.

Table 12.1. Advertising Media

Media Advertising	Web Pages
Newspapers	Banners
Magazines	Video/Film
Trade Journals	Promotional Videos/DVDs and Films
Specialized Publications	
Brochure Advertising	Outdoor
Media Guides/Game-Day Programs	Posters
	Point of Purchase Displays
Specialized Literature	Billboards
Broadcast Media	Transit/Transportation Advertising
Television (local, regional, national)	
Radio (local, regional, national)	Signage Arena and Sports Facilities
	Special Events
Exhibitions	Aerial Advertising
Special Events	Mobile Billboards
Trade Show Displays	Movie Theater Advertising
Internet	

Table 12.2. **Media: Advantages and Disadvantages**

Newspapers
- Advantages: Geographic selectivity and flexibility, short-term advertiser commitments, year-round readership, high individual market coverage, short lead time.
- Disadvantages: Little demographic sensitivity, limited color capabilities, low pass-along rate, may be expensive.

Magazines
- Advantages: Good reproduction, color, demographic selectivity, regional selectivity, local market selectivity, relatively long advertising life.
- Disadvantages: Long-term commitments, slow audience buildup, lack of urgency, long lead time.

Radio
- Advantages: Low cost, immediacy of message, can be scheduled on short notice, highly portable, short-term commitments, entertainment carryover.
- Disadvantages: No visual treatment, short advertising life, high frequency required to generate comprehension, background sound.

Television
- Advantages: Ability to reach a wide, diverse audience, low cost per thousand, creative opportunities, immediacy of message, entertainment carryover.
- Disadvantages: Short life of message, skepticism about claims, high campaign costs, long-term advertiser commitments, long lead times required for production.

Outdoor Media
- Advantages: Repetition, moderate cost, flexibility, geographic sensitivity.
- Disadvantages: Short message, lack of demographic selectivity, high noise level distracting audience.

Internet
- Advantages: Fastest growing medium, reach narrow target audience, short lead time required for creating Web-based advertising, moderate cost.
- Disadvantages: Difficult to measure ad effectiveness and return on investment, ad exposure relies on click-through from banner ads, not all consumers have access to the Internet.

Camp Tip

Because advertising costs money, develop a camper profile. Knowing the potential campers is the first step in reaching them.

With these customer profile questions answered through marketing planning, the question of how to contact and persuade the customer becomes easier. In the simplest terms, one must know the current and potential customers before one can promote and communicate with them. After determining who the customer is, match the financial resources up with the most effective advertising tools the camp can afford. Hopefully, the camp's financial budget will support those tools.

A.I.D.A

Once connected with the camp's potential customers, creativity comes into play. Advertising (and all forms of marketing communication) should follow AIDA.

- *Attention.* The advertising tools utilized must first gain the customers' attention. In a majority of all advertising, one has a precious few seconds to achieve this. Since people are saturated with a continued bombardment of advertising, if one does not catch and grab the potential camper's attention immediately, he or she will move on.

- *Interest.* After successfully getting customers' attention, the advertisement must seize their interest. In other words, once their attention is grabbed, it must be held until the message is delivered.

- *Desire.* Subsequent to getting prospective campers' attention and interest, one must get them to desire the camp's education service. If the advertising is imaginative and directed toward the camp's target market, developing the desire for the service is the next step in the AIDA progression.

Table 12.3. **Sample Advertising Media Mix for a Summer Sports Camp**

A possible advertising media mix that could be used by a camp can include the following:

- sports-specific journals (local, regional, national);
- local publications (newspaper's camp editions, city magazines, community newsletters, etc.);
- athletic organization game-day programs, media guides, alumni periodicals, etc.;
- TV and radio (possible piggybacking on athletic organization broadcasts as well as local targeted television and audio stations);
- signage (banners at athletic organization events and community activities that have a high percentage of targeted potential participants);
- posters and billboards; and
- flyers and pamphlets.

- *Action.* This is the final stage. If A, I, and D are accomplished, getting the camper to purchase and support the camp should fall in line.

In today's world, the concept of creativity in advertising is crucial. If one wants to achieve AIDA, the creative advertising work must be focused on what the customers are interested in. Actual inspiration for ideas typically can come from unstructured techniques such as brainstorming and free association methods.

> **Camp Tip**
> AIDA takes creativity. Creativity can be an internal trait or it can be inspired by others. It is possible not to have creativity as part of one's personal make-up. If this is the case, then recruit people with the gift of creativity. As a camp administrator, a well-defined strength can be the ability to recognize and accept one's own weaknesses.

Summer Camp Brochures

Typically, one of a summer sports camp's primary advertising instruments is the camp brochure. While it has multiple functions (information, registration, etc.), it can and often is the principal communication tool with the target market. Figure 12.1 provides a breakdown of a summer sports camp brochure. One note: This template applies to both hardcopy and electronic brochures.

Cover
This component of a summer sports camp brochure should be as dynamic and eye catching as possible. Remember, the camp brochure is as much a marketing tool as it is an informational document.

Bios
Biographies should be provided on all key clinicians and instructors. The biographies should promote the individual's sport-specific accomplishments and experience.

Camp Breakdown
This is the primary segment of the brochure. There should be a clean delineation of

- dates,
- times,
- locations,
- levels,
- session learning objectives, and
- format and costs.

This component should be readable and as comprehensive as possible.

Registration Form
On the inside back cover of the brochure there should be a complete registration form.

The registration form should incorporate

- a section for participant information (name, address, phone, email, educational institution, etc.),
- check-off list with prices on the camp sessions that the participant will attend,
- payment information and schedules, and
- return address, or web address for signing up online.

Mailing Section
The brochure should be able to be mailed directly to potential participants. On the outside back cover, a return address and open mailing address section should be designed. When a request comes in for camp information, fill in the potential participant's address, place a stamp in the top right corner, staple, and send.

Figure **12.1. Summer Camp Brochure Template**

Other tips for the construction of a brochure:

1. Whether a trifold, bifold, or 8 X 10 booklet, the design and professional presentation of the brochure should be a top priority. The brochure is an explicit reflection on the camp (and, if applicable, athletic organization).

2. Prior to finalizing the brochure, the promotional document should be examined by the compliance officer of the athletic organization for any possible sport/athletic organization violations (NCAA, NAIA, High School Athletic Association, etc.). The brochure should be signed off by this individual.

3. If designing a camp brochure is outside one's expertise, and one is employed by or has access to a college or university athletic department, contracting a member of a sports information department is a significant alternative. These individuals have hands-on experience in drafting athletic program catalogues, which are much more complex than a camp brochure.

4. Consistency is a crucial element in developing an appealing camp brochure. Format, fonts, spacing, colors, etc., should all be uniform and complementary.

5. Triple-check all final prints before circulating the camp brochure to the target market. Errors, such as grammatical, spelling, and

sentence structure, show a lack of concern for detail. This is not a good marketing message.

Direct Marketing

Direct marketing is "any advertising activity which creates and exploits a direct relationship between you and your prospect or customer as an individual."[8] The key to contacting large numbers of individual camper prospects though direct marketing techniques comes from advances in technology and is known in business as *mass customization*. Mass customization enables mass-produced products (or in this case, *promotional communications*) to be customized for each individual.

Another important aspect of direct marketing is the development of an extensive database of *qualified target market customers*. The operative word in the last sentence is *qualified*. While a phone book may be a possible database of potential customers, it probably would not be a qualified, targeted database for a summer sports camp. How does one find a suitable database to use for direct marketing purposes? Such a database should come from the market segmentation process discussed earlier in the book.

To review:

1. Identify the camp's overall market.

2. Break down the market into segments of people with similar needs, wants, characteristics, and purchasing behavior.

3. Select the most appropriate segment(s) on which to focus efforts.

4. Profile the selected segment to find the most efficient way to contact prospects.

As mentioned, direct marketing techniques are managed through databases. There are two ways to gain access to a database. The first and more difficult way is to construct one's own. To do so, find current and potential campers and their parents, design the system of data retrieval and use, and then catalog and computerize the list. The second option is to use a database that already exists. Sources for databases that already exist are plentiful, and through the ever-growing power of computers, the number of relevant lists available is increasing. Whether it is a geographic, demographic, psychographic, or behavioral database, never forget that the camp's segment profile will determine which one (or ones) to use.

As with all forms of communication, direct marketing involves planning and research as well as creativity, target market appeal, AIDA, and production and distribution methods. Whatever direct marketing techniques are selected to reach the target market segment, one must know the marketing concepts behind each technique.

It would serve a camp administrator well to do a cost-benefit analysis to see if direct marketing is necessary and financially possible. The investment of time and money in putting together a direct marketing plan is extensive. Once again, the main factor that determines whether to use any promotional tool is the customer. Through analysis, if direct marketing is proven to be effective and the financial resources of

Camp Tip

A danger in direct mailing is saturation. Monitor the amount of direct contacts the camp has with its supporters. If the camp exceeds acceptable direct contacts with its potential customers, not only will the message be disregarded, but it might instill a negative opinion of the camp in the eyes of the customer.

the camp can support a direct marketing campaign, then it is a powerful and focused promotional instrument.

Sales Promotions

Sales promotion is defined as

> non-personal marketing activities other than advertising, personal selling, and public relations that stimulate consumer purchasing and dealer effectiveness. . . . [S]ales promotion has emerged as an integral part of the promotional mix. Promotion now accounts for close to half as many marketing dollars as are spent on advertising, and promotional spending is rising faster than ad spending. Sales promotion consists of forms of promotion such as coupons, product samples, and rebates that support advertising and personal selling.[9]

These devices are used to create awareness and to stimulate sales. Some of the possible sales promotion techniques that could be utilized by a camp include family discounts, early registration coupons, and multiple-camp rebates. From a camp administrative perspective, the creativity that goes into sales promotion can be rich and rewarding.

The following section covers some basic sales promotion techniques along with their relative cost and time considerations.

Sales Promotional Techniques

Price-oriented programs seek to reduce the consumer's real cost per unit in some way, e.g.,:

> (a) cents-off coupons . . . (b) mail–in refunds or rebates.
> *Premiums:* Another item is given away or offered at an attractive price if a certain number of units are purchased.
> *Tie-Ins:* Similar to premiums, but involves joint promotion of two items . . . . Typically, the two parties share the cost of the promotion.
> *Continuity Program:* A reward is given in recognition of continuing relationships.
> *Contest/Sweepstakes:* Used to generate excitement about product.[10]

Once again, it must be stated that while cost and time are important considerations in choosing a sales promotion, the most critical factor is the camp's target market and the market's openness to certain sales promotion techniques. No matter how effective a sales promotional method could be in terms of time and cost, if it does not stimulate or support sales, it will squander camp resources.

Personal Selling

Personal selling is one-on-one, face-to-face discussions between camp representatives and prospective campers and their parents. The benefits of a successful sales call can be enormous. Not only can a personal sales call close an immediate sale, but it also

Camp Tip

Sales promotions (if allowed by the athletic organization's governing body regulations) should be controlled. Sales promotions should be manipulated to stimulate demand over limited periods. If sales promotions are overused and expected, then they become a permanent component of a camp's pricing strategy rather than a promotional tool to increase sales.

establishes a personal rapport for future encounters. This, in turn, can lead to positive word of mouth networking that creates more sales.

Essentially, every marketing and advertising textbook goes through a step-by-step procedure to make a sales presentation or to close a personal sale. While there are slight variations in the steps and content, in order to be successful, each sales person must have certain general attitudes.

Attitude is of course the ultimate characteristic that distinguishes the superstar from the also ran. A positive and enthusiastic attitude will become the major ingredient not only in developing relationships but also in winning a great deal of new business and earning your clients' trust, which will lead to recommendations and referrals. A positive attitude is the single most desirable attribute of a successful sales person.[11]

The following is one of the many step-by-step procedures that can be used in making a sales presentation and closing a sale. It should be noted that this step-by-step presentation template is appropriate to individuals and groups. For groups, a more formal presentation may be required.

1. Prospecting
2. Preapproach
3. Approach
4. Presentation
5. Trial close
6. Determine objections
7. Meet objections
8. Trial close
9. Close
10. Follow-up[12]

Personal selling goes beyond a broad promotional tool. Personal selling has been referred to as a business skill that takes hard work and vast experience to master. It is composed of

- building relationships, both short term and long term;
- providing skillful demonstrations;
- personal recommendations;
- showmanship and presentation dynamics;
- tactical negotiation;
- networking and campaigning; and
- role playing and performing.

Camp Tip

The concept of AIDA is appropriate for all communication tools, especially sales promotions. Sales promotions, to be valuable, must concentrate totally on the group and its tendencies. If one truly knows who the camp's potential customers are, think through what sales promotion techniques will grab their attention and get them to take action.

> **Camp Tip**
>
> As discussed, personal selling, as it relates to camps, is geared toward relationship building and educating prospective participants as to what the sports camp is all about. Two areas of personal selling to control are (1) having knowledgeable associates selling the camp and (2) finding new customers. Anyone and everyone can assist in the personal selling of a camp venture as long as they have a thorough knowledge of the operation. To ensure this knowledge base, training and open communication should be employed.

For a camp administrator to take advantage of this method in camp promotion and communication, one must set aside the time to appreciate and understand the process as well as rehearse and practice its use.

Special Note on Personal Selling: Knowing your camp is important when selling it to campers and parents. Being upfront on the camp's structure, philosophy, competitive environment, and overall program is a requirement for customer satisfaction. It must be emphatically stated that not all sports camps are right for all potential participants. During the personal selling process—as well as all marketing communication tactics—this element should be stressed. Under no circumstance should misinformation be allowed to be communicated to potential participants and their parents or guardians. Everyone involved with personal selling must be instructed that if they are asked a question that they are unsure of how to answer, they must either find out the answer and communicate it back to the potential camper or parent or they must refer the question and potential camper and parent to a knowledgeable camp administrator.

To encourage personal selling, a sales commission program could be employed. For every camp admission sold, a percentage or sales commission would be earned. Different sales would generate unique incentives. For example, a sale of a team for a team camp or tournament would generate a different commission than a sale of a singular specialty camp.

Publicity and Public Relations

The concepts of publicity and public relations have numerous definitions that vary in substance and structure. For the purpose of this book, the following is a description of the fundamental nature of publicity and public relations for summer sports camps.

Publicity

Promotional tool in which information about a company or product is transmitted by general mass media. . . . [P]ublicity is free. Marketers usually have little control over publicity, but because it is presented in a news format, consumers often regard it as objective.

Public Relations

Company-influenced publicity directed at building goodwill with the public or dealing with unfavorable events. . . . A firm will try to establish goodwill with customers (and potential customers) by performing and publicizing its public-service activities.[13]

A core consideration in these definitions is the need to develop and preserve a highly regarded public image. This corporate identity (in this case, camp identity) is not only for the way people think of the camp now, but also for the way they imagine the camp in the future. If the camp's impression is one that produces upbeat, positive feelings, the camp's public relations foundation is sound and can support the operation. If the current camp image has little or no response, either positive or negative, associated with it, one can look at this situation from a clean-slate viewpoint, and the camp's public relations outlook is an opportunity for growth. Finally, and regrettably, if the camp's image provokes negative feelings, one will need to stem the tide of disapproving opinions and start the lengthy process of building a new picture for the camp.

The advantages of public relations are considerable:

1. **Credibility.** Because public relations communications are not perceived in the same light as advertising—that is, the public does not realize the organization either directly or indirectly paid for them—they tend to have more credibility.

2. **Cost.** In both absolute and relative terms, the cost of public relations is very low, especially when the positive effects are considered.

3. **Avoidance of clutter.** Because they are typically perceived as news items, public relations messages are not subject to the clutter of ads.

4. **Lead generation.** Information about technological innovations, medical breakthroughs, and the like results almost immediately in a multitude of inquires. These inquires may give the firm some quality sales leads.

5. **Ability to reach specific groups.** Because some products appeal to only small market segments, it is not feasible to engage in advertising and/or promotion to reach them. If the firm does not have the financial capabilities to engage in promotional expenditures, the best way to communicate to these groups is through public relations.

6. **Image building.** Effective public relations helps to develop a positive image for the organization.[14]

As with most camp items, public relations and publicity need a formal plan. For sports camps it should be clarified that public relations have two distinct elements. The first is known as *campaign public relations* and the second is *perpetual public relations.* Public relations campaigns are one-time projects with a fixed timeframe. Perpetual public relations is a continual process set up (through a public relations system) to operate as long as the summer sports camp is functioning. Campaigns are associated with intensive development efforts and attempts to reach identified goals, while perpetual public relations systems are characterized by long-term relationships and consistency.

Camp Tip

Always be mindful of the camp's public relations image. Damage to the camp's image can be difficult to repair. As the camp's visible leader, spend time developing positive relations with key media personnel. Goodwill and trust are earned, so be patient and persistent.

Table 12.4. P.R., Media, and Communication Avenues

Electronic/Technological

Internet blogs

Newsletters

Industry-wide electronic publications

Direct electronic communication

Athletic program web pages

Chat rooms/Discussion boards

Search engines

Video teleconferencing

E-conferencing

Social media (Facebook, Twitter, YouTube)

Traditional methods

Public relations community events/ Sponsorships

Public appearances (top internal personnel)

Press releases and press kits

Correspondence inserts/Billing inserts

Traditional advertising media (TV, radio, periodicals, direct mailing, etc.)

News stories

Interviews

TV and press conferences

Brochures and internal fliers

Paraphernalia (cups, hats, t-shirts, pens, etc.)

Note: The ultimate goal of selecting the right media and communication techniques is to generate positive word-of-mouth for the camp.

Table 12.4 presents media avenues to pursue when developing a public relations promotional program.

Technology and Promotions

Web-based technology is an economical way to promote a camp. Not only can the entire contents of the camp brochure be included on the web page, but an expanded and more in-depth description of the summer sports camp operations can be built in. A portfolio of camp pictures, camp structure and learning objectives, facility directions, participant requirements, and contact information can be included in the web page's shell. Additionally, all camp forms can be placed into the web page as downloadable attachments. If the camp accepts credit cards, a payment link could be included.

Direct mail can use technology like emails to generate tremendous marketing communication benefits for a summer sports camp. Once again the concept of mass customization is defined as "the ability of a company to prepare on a mass basis individually designed products, services, programs and communications, to meet each customer's requirement."[15] The marketing communication model of mass customization is the production of large quantities of marketing communication emails but tailoring them for each individual customer. The key to utilizing this strategy is finding relevant email listings and the construction of an adaptable email template.

Social media has become an extremely viable tool for marketing communications through applications like Twitter and Facebook. While the "nuts and bolts" of establishing accounts with various social media sites differs, a vital component of their application is in the summer sports camp's use and

© Pressureua | Dreamstime.com

maintenance of these tools. Social media is only as valuable as it is used. For example, posting camp updates and marketing communication messages once a month lessens the power of this type of communication media to the point where it is a non-factor. Simply stated, social media needs continuous attention for it to have an impact on a camp. If the camp's human resources allow, the designation of a social media supervisor who is in charge of the camp's technology communication could be a valuable camp addition.

ENDNOTES

1. Perreault, W. D., & McCarthy, E. J. (2006). *Essentials of marketing: A global-managerial approach* (10th edition), pp. 318-319. New York, NY: McGraw-Hill/Irwin.

2. Stone, M. A., & Desmond, J. (2007). *Fundamentals of marketing,* pp. 317-318. New York, NY: Routledge.

3. Shank, M. D. (2005). *Sports marketing: A strategic perspective* (3rd edition), pp. 290-291. Upper Saddle River, NJ: Prentice Hall.

4. Peterson, R. (2007). *Principles of marketing,* Section 6. Chandi Chowk, Delhi: Delhi Global Media.

5. Madura, J. (2007). *Introduction to business* (4th edition), p. 529. Mason, OH: Thompson South-Western.

6. Callen, B. (2010). *Manager's guide to marketing, advertising, and publicity,* p. 174. New York, NY: McGraw-Hill Professional.

7. Lamb, C. W., Hair, J. F., & McDaniel, C. (2003). *Essentials of marketing* (3rd edition), p. 449. Mason, OH: Thompson South-Western.

8. Bird, D. (2007). *Common sense direct and digital marketing,* p. 17. London, EG: Kogan Page.

9. Boone, L. E., & Kurtz, D. L. (2006). *Contemporary business 2006,* p. 463. Mason, OH: Thompson South-Western.

10. Lal, R., Quelch, J. A., & Kasturi Rangan, V. (2005). *Marketing management,* p. 267. New York, NY: McGraw-Hill/Irwin.

11. Denny, R. (2009). *Successful selling skills,* p. 9. London, England: Kogan Page.

12. Futrell, C.M. (2011). *ABC's of relationship selling through service* (11th edition), p. 204. New York, NY: McGraw-Hill/Irwin.

13. Griffin, R. W., & Ebert, R. J. (2004). *Business* (7th edition), p. 379. Upper Saddle River, NJ: Prentice Hall.

14. Belch, G. E., & Belch, M. A. (2009). *Advertising and promotion: An integrated marketing communication perspective* (8th edition), pp. 571-572. Boston, MA: McGraw Hill/Irwin.

15. Kotler, P. (2003). *Marketing management* (11th edition), p. 282. Upper Saddle River, NJ: Prentice Hall.

SECTION VI:

RISK MANAGEMENT AND CAMP OPERATIONS

One of the central goals of this book is to enable readers to become critical thinkers about camp administration. No topic exemplifies this core idea as much as *risk management*. The camp administrator's core concentration must be a philosophy of camper safety. Camper safety can be maintained through monitoring risks to facilities, equipment, and personnel. Camp safety is kept through the committed monitoring of contractual agreements and the regulation of external risks through insurance. No matter what level of risk a camp administrator accepts, he or she must be as thorough and detail oriented as possible. Additionally, a camp administrator needs to enlist others in the process of risk management. The better the collective input, the better the potential hazards can be managed.

As discussed throughout this book, the most important element of a summer sports camp is the value of the instruction and overall management of the operation. While the administration functions prior to a camp are critical in developing a camp venture, the actual day-in, day-out quality of instruction has the most impact on a camp's current and future success. No matter what the sport, the intensity or level, and camp structure, all effort should be made to provide the customer (both parents and campers) with the finest conceivable product: sports instruction. This is accomplished through teamwork, strong leadership, sound daily organization, and inspiring sports-specific instructional techniques. If the quality delivered to the customer is exceptional, the likelihood for future growth is promising. Unfortunately, if the camp's management and leadership does not convey quality, the opposite will be realized.

Properly shutting down a camp operation is as significant as setting up a camp. In fact, these two actions are often connected when it comes to a camp that is an ongoing venture. A "clean" shut down can also include continuing activities that cultivate a camp's future operation. The significance of this stage is vital in relation to all other camp-related actions. To overlook it could be catastrophic to any possible future the camp might have.

13

Risk Management

INTRODUCTION

The issue of risk management in camps is a very detailed and specialized legal and financial field. However, it is an aspect of business about which camp personnel should be aware and have a fundamental working knowledge. Camp administrators work with people in a service industry that is extremely physical and dynamic. Child safety is involved, numerous facilities are utilized, and camp operations typically have a wide range of clinicians and support staff that require supervision. It is necessary to constantly evaluate the camp's environment and make suitable decisions to reduce the chance of risk and loss.

Camp Tip

When dealing with risk and risk management, never take for granted that all parties involved with the camp know the consequences of risk management.

RISK AND RISK MANAGEMENT DEFINED

The most reasonable explanation of risk and risk management is as follows:

> Risk needs to be understood across a continuum from those events that present the potential for damage to the business strategy, to those that compose uncertainties implicit in the execution of that strategy, to those that must be embraced in order to achieve the goals of the organization. Expanding this definition of risk management in this manner has the potential to engage the entire organization . . . and assess the risks that are not only to be avoided but also embraced in the service of achieving the goals of an organization.[1]

Another key element in risk and risk management relates to *losses*. From this word, one might think of litigation through gross negligence. However, lawsuits can happen over the slightest and most improbable incidents. Let us be honest in judging our culture by stating that we exist in a "sue-happy" society. Outrageous legal court settlements are commonplace, whether warranted or not. Camp administrators are as vulnerable as anyone.

The concept of risk management goes beyond gross negligence. Throughout her 1997 text titled *Sports Business Management,* Lori Miller categorizes general business risks into the following environmental segments:

1. Facilities and equipment risk

2. Personnel risk

3. Contract related risk

4. External risk[2]

If camp administrators adopt her groupings and fashion them toward their individual camps, it will give them the basis for approaching and reducing organizational and personal liabilities. Will risk ever be eliminated? No. Risk is inherent in uncertainty. However, the objective should be to influence and manage as many variables as possible so that the likelihood of a dangerous and liable occurrence is diminished.

FACILITY AND EQUIPMENT RISK

In reviewing possible facility and equipment risks, a camp administrator must first think of all the worst-case situations and, around them, all potential problems. One must always ask, "What is the most catastrophic scenario?" In other words, a camp administrator must be a constant and deliberate observer of potential disasters. Facilities and equipment deal with the physical aspects of a camp. They are physical objects that one's senses (sight, hearing, touch, and smell) can examine and evaluate. When assessing the condition, layout, and safety of existing or potential facilities and equipment, it is advisable to set aside separate, free time prior to facility and/or equipment usage that utilizes one's senses to evaluate the situation. Once scheduled camp activities begin, a camp administrator's heightened attention is more on those activities than the surroundings. As a result, a walkthrough of a camp's facilities and equipment should be completed considerably in advance to avoid any other distractions. For example, before starting a camp session, have the facility crew set up the gym, field, or facility according to the precise camp requirements a day before starting. Do a safety walk-through with the camp's administrators, clinicians, and staff. Use the five human senses and ask questions:

- How does the ground (floor) feel? Is it clear of miscellaneous items or does it need more attention?

- Is the light adequate to conduct instruction sessions?

- What is the facility temperature? Is there proper circulation?

- Is there proper spacing around the participation areas? If not, are the walls or boundaries padded to avoid injury?
- What is the condition of the operational equipment? Is it in good working order?
- What is the condition of the locker rooms? Is there an unhealthy smell? Are the locker rooms area secure?
- Does the current design of the field/court/gym minimize the chance for injury?
- Where will the campers obtain water? Could there unintentionally be a hazardous situation caused by its placement and distribution?

In 1985, Neil Dougherty and Diane Bonanno presented an outstanding outline for examining most facility and equipment risks in their text *Management Principles in Sport and Leisure Services.* Their specific guidelines for a safe environment:

I. Develop and implement regular inspection and maintenance schedules for all facilities and equipment.

   A. Assign individual responsibilities.

   B. Establish procedures for correcting deficiencies.

II. Be sure any new facility exceeds all applicable safety standards. Give great attention to such details as surfacing, free area around courts and fields, lighting, and the presence of obstacles or dangerous protrusions on walls.

III. Be sure all equipment meets or exceeds applicable safety standards and is designed properly for the purpose in which it will be used.

IV. When equipment must be installed, give careful attention to the question of who will do the installing. The use of local staff in the installation process often voids any guarantee/warranty that may exist and, in certain instances, may absolve the manufacture of liability in the event of product failure.

V. Provide safety equipment for all participants and require its use. Post reminders for staff and for the participants to guarantee their awareness of the importance of protective equipment.

   Dougherty and Bonanno go on to say:

> Administrators must guarantee the safety and appropriateness of the area in which the activity takes place and also the safety of any equipment used. . . [T]here is a clear obligation to eliminate any environmental conditions that may interfere with the safety of the participants.[3]

Prior to the beginning of the camp, an official meeting should be conducted with all maintenance and set-up/breakdown crews. The meetings should clearly confirm expectations concerning set-up standards, maintenance and cleaning, and camp breakdown. Walkthroughs with maintenance crews, in combination with meetings, should be conducted to visualize the requirements of camp operations. In addition to this process, it is advisable to construct standardized checklists and time schedules to reinforce the importance of each task's completion.

The total number of questions to be asked will be based on the condition of the operational equipment or facility and the summer sports camp personnel's sensitivity to risk. Obviously, the newer the facility or equipment, the less one should worry about its mechanical condition rather than its continual upkeep. Even the newest facilities become hazardous without appropriate maintenance.

What if the camp is dealing with a confined budget and older facilities and equipment? Document (in writing) all possible problems and concerns and give copies to the controlling organization's supervisors from whom the camp may be leasing the facility. One's concerns should be absolutely clear and as professional as possible. Declare facts, be very clear, and eliminate all impulsive, emotional responses. Also, supply solutions to all conclusions brought forth in the disclosure. Copy reports to all parties concerned. As unfortunate as this process may appear, by discussing any potential dangers, one will have taken steps to limit personal liability. Does this imply that the camp administrator ignores potential problems and conducts activities as though there is nothing wrong? No. Sit down with the camp's personnel and candidly discuss potential facility and equipment risks. Make everyone mindful of the circumstances and emphasizes a safety-sensitive theme in the camp.

PERSONNEL RISK

A service is defined as "a deed performed by one party for another. . . . [A] service is experienced, used or consumed. . . . [S]ervices are not physical—they are intangible."[4] Camp administrators provide assistance and expertise to their employees so that they, in turn, can furnish the final consumer (camper) with a service (sports education). In other words, the nature of the camp involves dealing with and training people internally so that they can produce externally. This type of intense training requires personnel policies and procedures to minimize risks.

In a model world, all men and women would work in an ideal environment of teamwork and civility. Personal and professional conflicts between a summer sports camp's personnel would be nonexistent. Unfortunately, we do not live or work in an ideal world. As a camp administrator, one needs to cultivate, motivate, and influence people, such as clinicians, administration, and staff to achieve the camp's mission. This is the substance of HR management (Chapters 8 and 9).

Some of the obstacles facing business managers dealing with people include the following:

- Fair hiring and recruiting policies
- Equal pay for equal work
- Sexual harassment
- Discriminatory hiring and employment practices
- Wrongful termination disputes
- Promotion and preferential treatment
- Valid, reliable evaluation methods
- Employee job safety

Do these uncertainties challenge a camp administrator? Absolutely. In fact, administrators are confronted with these issues from two separate work groups: campers and employees. There are some key, common sense measures a camp administrator can adopt to create a more risk-averse HR system. First of all, get educated (or re-educated) in relevant personnel topics. Browse through human resource texts, attend human resource seminars (e.g., sexual harassment, discrimination, OSHA workshops), and revisit the camp's strategic HR plan. Second, develop a camp manual that spells out specific rules for the camp and all its stakeholders. A sample camp manual template is provided in Figure 13.1.

Develop a relationship with the camp's personnel, even if it is through scheduled verbal meetings. Give them an opportunity to voice their feelings and beliefs about any aspect of the camp. Finally, maintain a file for each camp member. Document all important material for future reference. If possible, have dates, times, and specific items recorded for reference purposes. This, in turn, can reduce any future disagreements and contradictions.

Mission Statement	Administrators
Long-Term Objectives (3 to 5 Years)	Head Clinician
	Assistant Clinicians
Short-Term Objectives to Reach Long-Term Goals	Trainers
	Staff
Camp Rules and Policies	Other Related Members
Disciplinary Policies	Personnel Evaluation System
Job Responsibilities	

Figure 13.1. **Summer Sports Camp Manual Outline**

CONTRACT-RELATED RISK

The importance of contracts for sports camps can be summed up in the following excerpt:

> A contract is a promise or a set of promises for the breach in which the law gives remedy, or the performance of which the law in some way recognizes as duty. Put simply, a contract is a legally binding agreement between two or more parties who agree to perform or to refrain from performing some act now or in the future. Generally, contract disputes arise when there is a promise of future performance. If the contractual promise is not fulfilled, the party who made it is subject to the sanctions of the court. That party may be required to pay damages for failing to perform the contractual promise; in limited instances, the party may be required to perform the promised act.[5]

Camp Tip

Once again, to minimize disorder, keep all camp business and contracts separate from normal athletic program operations (if applicable). Contracts for insurance, staff employment, state registrations, camper registration, camper insurance, and medical documentation, and checking accounts are among some of the contracts that should be formalized and retained. Most sports governing bodies require detailed record maintenance for sport-related camps. Make sure all contractual forms are available in case of a spot audit.

Contracts deal categorically with rights, responsibilities, and remuneration between participants. The fundamental requirements for a contractual agreement (whether formal and written, or informal) are listed below.

Requirements for a Contract

Agreement: An agreement to form a contract includes an offer and acceptance. One party must offer to enter into a legal agreement, and another party must accept the terms of the offer.

Consideration: Any promise made by parties must be supported by legal, sufficient and bargained-for consideration (something of value received or promised, such as money, to convince a person to make a deal).

Contractual Capacity: Both parties entering into the contract must have the contractual capacity to do so; the law must recognize them as possessing characteristics that qualify them as competent parties.

Legality: The contract's purpose must accomplish some goal that is legal and not against public policy.[6]

Additionally, for the contract to be enforceable, the following two elements are raised as defenses to the enforceability of an otherwise valid contract.

Voluntary consent. The consent of both parties must be voluntary. For example, if a contract was formed as a result of fraud, undue influence, mistake, or duress, the contract may not be enforceable.

Form: The contract must be in whatever form the law requires; for example, some contracts must be in writing to be enforceable.[7]

It is important to note that once these six criteria are met, an oral contract is just as binding as a written one. The obvious disadvantage is that oral agreements are much more difficult to enforce exactly because it is more difficult to prove their existence. That is why it is strongly recommended to formalize all contracts in writing.

Contracts can be applied widely to minimize personal and camp risks. Unless one is a contract lawyer, it is important to state that the more critical a contractual arrangement, the more fitting it is to involve an independent specialist in contract law. For example, if a camp is in a position to negotiate an employment contract for a high-profile clinician (which most administrators would regard as a somewhat considerable employment item), it is advisable to get a contract lawyer to counsel one as to the rights and responsibilities of the contract. On the other hand, there are contractual arrangements that everyday camp operations do not need legal representation and advisement to execute. The following are a few examples.

Camp Purchasing

When dealing with vendors, it is sensible to obtain written quotes on all services and products when negotiating prices, quantities, and specifications. After both parties stipulate the services and products to be included, formal written contracts (and purchase orders if applicable) should be generated and approved by all parties. Keep copies of all documentation for future reference.

Personnel Travel

Maintain complete files for each trip planned and completed for out-of-town staff and clinicians. Files should consist of hotel contracts, rental vehicle contracts, flight receipts, and miscellaneous travel-related items. If the camp pays a travel contract in advance, make a copy of the check for proof of the camp's fulfillment of the two-sided agreement.

EXTERNAL RISK

External risks are elements outside the control of the operation and camp administrator. The question then arises: If the external risks are outside one's control, why do camp administrators need to acknowledge them or be worried with them? This is where the concept of adaptation versus control separates the successful, long-term operators from the day-to-day managers. One's managerial objective to minimize risk should be to adapt the camp to environmental elements that affect the operation but are out of one's immediate power to control or change.

Camp Tip

Oral contracts and agreements are just as binding as written contracts. To enforce oral contracts and agreements, with the permission of all parties, video tape the oral contract.

Camp Tip

With any substantial camp purchase, have the quotes and estimates evaluated by the camp's legal counsel. Specify all the camp's purchasing requirements and have the legal advisor verify that these stipulations are included in the contractual purchase agreement.

Camp Tip

Have sufficient copies of all individual travel contracts available for camp staff/clinician traveling to and from camp. This can provide individuals with travel safety as well as planning flexibility.

In planning for external risk, one must be future oriented. For example, if the country is suddenly in an economic downturn that alters the camp's operations, the most desirable strategy would be to anticipate this direction and retool the camp in advance to compensate and adapt. Unfortunately, some dilemmas are simply unpredictable. The key element in successfully managing these circumstances is to try to forecast whether they are stable and likely to remain or fleeting and likely to change. If a camp administrator can foresee the issue becoming a permanent trend, then he or she needs to adapt the camp's operations as quickly as possible and get out in front of the situation. Another solution to unforeseen events is to have an insurance arrangement that can protect the camp, campers, facilities, and so on.

GENERAL INSURANCE STRATEGY

The use of insurance, for all levels of operation, not just external risk, is crucial in today's camp environment. The following is a checklist on insurance selection and strategies:

- Never assume you are covered; always check your insurance coverage.
- Check your insurance policy at least twice a year for changes and to be sure you still have adequate coverage.
- File a report as soon as it happens and submit a proper claim to the insurance company.
- Anyone involved in an activity outside their job jurisdiction or areas of control may seek to secure more personal liability coverage.
- Be aware of potential hazards and report them to the necessary people or groups.
- Secure a short-term group accident policy to cover special activities when risk is foreseeable; analyze the liability aspect of your program or area and ensure adequate coverage in these areas.
- Have release forms. They may involve small liability problems because participants acknowledge the risk they are assuming and their voluntary participation in the program, but do not rely on them to solve any negligent actions
- Have participants in events obtain medical [histories].[8]

The level of insurance protection that the camp will need once again relates to the camp administrator's own personal outlook of risk and liability as well as the requirements of the operation.

SPORTS CAMP INSURANCE RECOMMENDATIONS

The following points are some but not all the possible considerations when determining a camp's insurance needs.

- First and foremost, if the camp is in an institutional setting, obtain in writing from the athletic administration the amount of liability coverage required by the organization. This initial level should be taken as a minimum requirement. Depending on the sport, the base amount of camp insurance coverage (per camper) can be increased. High risk/high impact sports should strongly consider expanding minimum coverage.

- If the camp is an independent venture, the camp should consult with the operation's legal counsel to establish coverage levels. Additionally, insurance coverage being carried by other comparable camp operations is a beneficial starting point.

- Make sure all contractual arrangements and certificates of coverage from the insurance carrier are in writing (hardcopy and e-copy) and examined by all relevant parties. Get final approval of insurance coverage, either by athletic department administrators or legal counsel, in writing as well.

- Do not assume coverage is all-inclusive. Be wary of potential loop holes in agreements. Triple-check dates of coverage, amounts of coverage, premiums paid, claims procedures, etc.

- Begin the search for and purchase of camp insurance early in the camp's developmental process. It is too important to delay it until the last moment.

- If transportation to off-site locations is provided for employees or campers, confirm that this is included in the camp's insurance policy. If not, separate coverage to off-site locations will need to be obtained. Additionally, any off-site coverage needs to be described well in advance of the camp's operations.

- Shop around for the best insurance policy or contract. Never sacrifice the quality of coverage for a better cost. Money saved now could be money paid later. To find possible insurance carriers, a good starting point is to network with local agencies or to perform a basic search engine investigation (Google, Yahoo, Bing, etc.).

- All active clinicians and staff members should be protected under the summer sports camp's insurance umbrella for their entire length of employment.

- Besides individual insurance coverage for employees and campers, consider the option of equipment and facility coverage at replacement cost, if applicable.

- Most insurance companies will ask for advanced premiums based on maximum potential attendance. Do not low-ball this number in an effort to save money. If the actual camp attendance is under the maximum number specified to the insurance carrier, post-camp refunds are normally provided. If your camp exceeds projected capacity, contact the insurance company immediately to obtain additional coverage.

© Jirsak | Dreamstime.com

INCIDENT TREATMENT

No matter how safety focused a camp is, no matter how reliable and immaculate the facility and equipment, and no matter what safety measures a camp has in place, accidents and injuries will happen. While accident and injury prevention is essential, pre-established and tested accident/injury procedures are just as crucial.

As much as possible, the steps to be taken at the time of the incident should be identified in advance. . . . Staff members in leadership positions should be given training and directions to cover points such as the following:

- Providing immediate care of individuals involved in the incident, both injured and uninjured
- Notifying one's supervisor or designated person as soon as possible
- Securing outside assistance, if necessary
- Writing a report on the incident, documenting as many facets as possible
- If serious, reporting to appropriate persons outside
- Diverting or organizing the persons not involved in the incident into other activities
- Referring media and determining who speaks for the organization[9]

The efficiency and success of accident/injury procedures falls squarely on the camp administrator. A camp administrator must do the following:

- Lead by example. If he or she takes accident/injury prevention and procedures seriously, all internal stakeholders will.
- Have a step-by-step accident/injury plan in place prior to any camp contacts or activities.
- Have a certified athletic trainer and medical staff in attendance for all camp activities. If this is not possible, the administrator should require that all camp personnel obtain Red Cross CPR and First Aid certifications.
- Require all camp members, especially clinicians and staff, to carry an accident/injury procedural card with them at all times. This card will have step-by-step measures to be taken in a crisis as well as emergency phone numbers. In addition, cell phones must be kept with all camp personnel at all camp activities. It is strongly suggested that preprogrammed emergency phone numbers be input into all cell phones.
- Keep all camp personnel notified at all times of the camp's schedule and activities.
- Get pre-approval from medical staff on all accident/injury procedures.

OTHER SAFETY AND RISK MANAGEMENT CONSIDERATIONS

The following are preventative measures to minimize a camp's risk and liability.

- Examine all possibilities; all scenarios necessitate some type of safety plan.
- Have all staff and clinicians safety trained for sports-identifiable injuries. Stress attendance in formal certifications and sanctioned training seminars.

- It is recommended that camp personnel obtain medical examinations.
- Know where medical and training staff are at all times throughout camp activities; minutes can be critical in minimizing long-term effects of accidents and injuries.
- *In no way consent* to nonapproved individuals participating in any of the camp's activities.
- Training and conditioning equipment must have the complete backing of the medical and training staff.
- Construct a complete safety procedural manual and circulate it to all internal camp stakeholders.
- Be unyielding on the appropriate use of all camp equipment. Additionally, under no circumstances improvise with equipment or use personally created contraptions.
- All external weather factors must outweigh a summer sports camp's events and proceedings.
- Stay trained in the most recent sports-specialized exercise and teaching techniques.
- Never allow coaches to sacrifice warm-up time for the camp athletes; doing so greatly increases the risk and endangers campers.
- Always avoid rushing campers back from injuries (no matter how much the camper pleads); have coaches follow all medical and training staff counsel.
- At no time should a camp administrator underestimate the significance of locker room maintenance and sanitation. Establish a timetable for cleaning and maintenance prior to all camp operations.
- Analyze the camp's sports-exclusive health hazards; research typical sports-specific issues.
- Most accidents and injuries arise from personal inattention and carelessness; make camp members and participants aware of this.
- If possible, have health management programs (physical conditioning, dieticians, personal counseling, etc.) accessible to all camp personnel and campers.

  Special Note on Sports Camp Risk Management: Once again, it should be forcefully stated that by no means should a camp administrator or anyone employed or associated with the camp consent to allowing a child or employee to participate in any event or activity without having his or her entire set of records. This could be interpreted as gross negligence and may be a cause for loss of protection under the camp's insurance carrier.

Another safety element of a camp that has rightly received mass media attention is the possibility of skin infections due to sports-related activities.

Because skin infections are preventable, a skin infection prevention plan should be in place at all facilities that host sports activities. Athletes should understand the plan and follow the precautions off the field as well. This plan should include:

1. providing sinks and liquid, antibacterial soap for washing hands and arms before and after practices and games; if a sink is not available, providing antibacterial gel or wipes that contain chlorhexidine gluconate (CHG) in order to provide long-term protection from bacteria;

2. providing clean and available showers for athletes, if at all possible;

3. ensuring sports equipment is cleaned and dried between practices and games;

4. assuring all wounds be covered with clean, dry bandages and checked by a physician if inflamed or painful;

5. eliminating the ability of athletes to share towels or other personal items; and

6. encouraging soiled clothing and towels to be taken home in separate bags for cleaning, not put back in lockers or bags with clean clothes.[10]

It is important to say again that camp safety and risk management are wide-ranging concepts. All camp facets (locker rooms, security, facilities and equipment, personnel interactions, etc.) are areas of camp concern. A useful camp risk management motto is to "expect the unexpected."

ENDNOTES

1. Sharon, B. (2006). Risk management: Worry about other things that need to go right. Business Credit, 108(8), 62–63.

2. Miller, L. K. (1997). Sports business management. Gaithersburg, MD: Aspen Publishing.

3. Dougherty, N. J., & Bonanno, D. (1985). Management principles in sport and leisure services, p. 136. Minneapolis, MN: Burgess Publishing.

4. Perreault, W. D., & McCarthy, E. J. (2007). Essentials of marketing: A global-managerial approach (11th edition), p. 195. New York, NY: McGraw-Hill/Irwin.

5. Jentz, G., Miller, R. L., & Cross, F. B. (2007). West's business law: Alternative edition, p. 189. Mason, OH: Thompson South-Western.

6. Clarkson, K. W., Miller, R. L., & Cross, F. B. (2012). Business law: Text and cases (12th edition), p. 208. Mason, OH: South-Western, Cengage Learning.

7. Ibid.

8. Sawyer, T. H., & Smith, O. (1999). The management of clubs, recreation and sport: Concepts and applications, p. 337. Champaign, IL: Sagamore Publishing.

9. Ball, A., & Ball, B. (2000). Basic camp management, pp. 176-177. Martinsville, IN: American Camping Association.

10. Back to school means back to sports: Prepare for and prevent common sports injuries. (2010). PR Newswire, para. 9 Retrieved from http://www.prnewswire.com/news-releases/back-to-school-means-back-to-sports-prepare-for-and-prevent-common-sports-injuries-100880509.html

CHAPTER

Management and Leadership

INTRODUCTION

This section relates to one critical camp item: quality. Quality is defined as "a product's or service's fitness for use, measured as durability, serviceability, style, ease of use, and dependability."[1] All camps want to call attention to these aspects of quality, especially in the areas of camp management and instruction. When it comes to delivering quality, a camp administrator should live by one philosophy: Do not meet the customer's quality expectations, exceed them. Simply stated, overwhelm the customer (i.e., parents and campers) with a professional, superior sports camp experience.

To achieve the objective of an exceptional camp, the operation must maximize the perceived and real value given to each and every camp participant. To achieve the value goal, one must emphasize the following:

- Highlight professionalism in all facets of the operation.
- Through strong management tactics, capitalize on all of the camp's resources and assets.
- Through sound administrative strategies, increase the staff and clinician's capabilities to use the camp's resources and assets efficiently.
- Provide the highest level of safety in all aspects of the operation.

- Establish and uphold the highest level of policies for all personnel. These policies go far beyond the tangible job descriptions and responsibilities.
- Cultivate an environment that promotes the development of sports-specific intellectual capital as well as innovative teaching techniques.

The benefits of a well-planned camp structure with sound daily camp management procedures are immeasurable. Positive word of mouth, strong social perception and community goodwill, greater market share, and an improved relationship with strategic partners are potential benefits of a well-operated camp.

Special Note: Because sports are diverse, this chapter of the book will need to talk in generalizations and universal concepts. In other words, with the considerable volume of camp options as well as the infinite number of management and leadership styles and approaches, it is difficult to discuss this topic for a specific circumstance. The concepts prescribed in this chapter, while generic in nature, can be adopted as is, modified for a specific camp, or ignored as a component of a summer sports camp operation.

DAILY SUMMER SPORTS CAMP ORGANIZATION

Camp Tip

While it is ideal to have all internal stakeholders attend daily planning meetings, at no time should campers be left unsupervised.

For greater structure and orderliness of the actual camp day, camp administrators/head clinicians should conduct a daily meeting for all camp staff, clinicians, and administrators every single camp day (whether morning, afternoon, or evening). The purpose of that meeting will be to review the camp's instructional plans and other critical camp items. Figure 14.1 is a detailed outline describing how to lead productive meetings. It should be mentioned that not all elements in the meeting template will apply to all sports camps. A camp administrator, along with the head clinician, will want to pick and choose parts of the outline and tailor their daily meeting accordingly.

DAILY INSTRUCTIONAL PLANS

In formal teacher education programs, the concept of instructional planning is a foundational concept. For camps, instructional planning relates directly to daily camp plans. In the text *The Act of Teaching,* Donald Cruickshank, Deborah Jenkins, and Kim Metcalf define instructional planning as "the process by which teachers decide what to teach, how to teach it, and how they will determine the extent to which students have learned and are satisfied."

They go on to say:

Thoughtful planning promotes learning because it causes us to take into account the diverse backgrounds, interests, and abilities of our students…a thoughtful plan is more likely to attract and maintain students' attention and to facilitate learning satisfaction given the instructional goals and available resources.[2]

Preparation Keys

1. Scheduling Meetings: Has the meeting been scheduled at the most convenient time for all the participants? Does the meeting conflict with any other camp activities?

2. Goals of Meetings: Are there goals for the meeting? Goals: to inform, to develop new ideas, to make decisions, to delegate, to persuade, to get collaboration.

3. Participants: Who gets selected to attend meetings? Are they key people who will be affected (or will affect) goals? Are they decision makers? Should there be separate meetings or break-out sessions for clinicians, staff, and administrators?

4. Site: Is the meeting site the best possible setting? Is the room adequate? Are the environmental elements under control? Is the furniture arranged appropriately? Is the furniture comfortable? Should participants have designated seats or is it festival seating? Will there be food and refreshments, a hospitality table?

5. Advanced Information: Is there an agenda of topics? How far in advance will participants need to have the meeting's agenda? Do presenters have advanced notice? Does your agenda have time allotments? Does the agenda's order have flow?

6. Technology (if applicable): Is it appropriate for the audience? Is it prepared in advance? Is there a contingency plan if it does not function?

Actual Meeting

Introduction and Meeting Ground Rules

- Roll call (if applicable)
- Facilitating introductions
- Goals and length (projected)
- Topics delineated
- Overall review of agenda

Body of Meeting

- Keep moving topics along
- Introduce presenters and not steal the show from them
- Avoid tangents: Lead group back onto original topic

- Conflict resolution (quickly and truthfully): Maintain order and standards
- Encourage participation from all member
- Reiterate any solutions to topics and get consensus

Meeting Termination

- Keep on schedule
- Have open question and answer time
- Provide overall summary of meeting: High points and agreed upon tasks/solutions
- Set time for follow-up meeting
- Thank participants for their time and contributions

Figure 14.1. **Leading Productive Meetings**

While building daily instructional plans can be time consuming, their advantages far outweigh any time issues involved in their development. Daily camp instructional planning benefits can include the following:

- Daily camp plans maximize a camp's instructional time (time being a fixed element) while minimizing any unproductive down time in a session. This then fosters a culture of professionalism and increased value for the participant.

- Having an all-inclusive instructional plan reduces anxiety among clinicians, staff, administrators, and participants.

- Camp plans help capacity utilization and avoid overlaps and double booking of camp areas.

- Instructional plans can incorporate contingency situations (e.g., for inclement weather) to avoid any confusion or wasted instruction opportunities.

- Daily instructional plans restate the camp's HR structure and chain of command.

- Instructional plans ensure a greater level of quality control on the various sessions offered.

The basis for a camp's daily planning is ultimately found in the camp's overall operational plan (big-picture goals) and in precamp orientation and training (small-picture actions). All instruction planning documents should be distributed like a playbook at orientation, and the daily meetings should be to restate and make adjustments. Depending on personnel, some aspects of the daily camp plan could have flexibility within the structure. Segments of the plan that have flexibility as well as elements that need to be followed as they are described should to be made clear to all relevant parties. The primary goal is to balance micromanagement with camp anarchy.

Special Note: Instructional plans should also contain nonsport-related activities such as rooming, meal times, and entertainment. While not instruction, these are critical elements for all personnel to know.

Sound camp instructional plans delineate and reaffirm the following six vital questions:

1. Who will conduct the instructional session?
2. What are the targeted instructional goals for the daily sessions?
3. Why is the instruction important?
4. Where will the instructional sessions take place?
5. When will the instructional sessions take place?
6. How will the instruction be conducted?

Figure 14.2 is a sample daily instructional plan format for an elite level women's volleyball day camp.

Camp Tip

Camp instructional plans should be distributed to all support staff and administrators, especially trainers and medical staff. These individuals will need to know at all times where every camper is and what activities they are doing.

Camp Tip

As a general rule, it is better to include more items into a camp's instructional plan than less to avoid unproductive down time. Ideally, the daily instructional plan will have the right amount of activities, for the right amount of participants, for the right amount of time.

The following is an illustration of a summer camp instructional plan format for an elite level women's volleyball day camp. The operational time period for the summer sports camp is four days at four hours a day (half-day sessions totaling 16 hours).

Group Name: _____

Lead Clinician: _____

Assistant Clinicians: _____

Facility Location: _____

Continued

Figure 14.2. **Sports Camp Instructional Plan Format**

1. **Skills to develop (increasing in complexity and difficulty: basic sport skills to multifaceted, composite play)**
   - Passing
   - Setting
   - Serving
   - Hitting/Attacking
   - Blocking
   - Defense
   - Serve Receive
   - Team Offensive Schemes
   - Team Defensive Schemes
   - Team Play

2. **Structured, hour-long sessions**
   - 0-10 minutes: Instruction of skill with demonstrations (group/entire camp)
   - 10-55 minutes: Continuous reinforcement of skills with drills and activities (breakout sessions in groups, pairs, or individuals)
   - 55-60 minutes: Collective break

3. **Overall camp outline**

DAY ONE
Pre-Instructional Warm-up and Stretching

Hour 1: Passing
Skill instruction and demonstrations
Listing and explanation of drills

Hour 2: Setting
Skill instruction and demonstrations
Listing and explanation of drills

Hour 3: Serving
Skill instruction and demonstrations
Listing and explanation of drills

Hour 4: Hitting/Attacking
Skill instruction and demonstrations
Listing and explanation of drills

Cool Down and Session Meeting

DAY TWO
Pre-Instructional Warm-up and Stretching

Hour 1: Blocking
Skill instruction and demonstrations
Listing and explanation of drills

Hour 2: Defense
Skill instruction and demonstrations
Listing and explanation of drills

Hour 3: Serve Receive
Skill instruction and demonstrations
Listing and explanation of drills

Hour 4: Team Offensive Schemes
Chalk talk
Offensive scheme walk-throughs
Listing and explanation of drills

Cool Down and Session Meeting

DAY THREE
Pre-Instructional Warm-up and Stretching

Hour 1: Team Defensive Schemes
Chalk talk
Defensive scheme walk-throughs
Listing and explanation of drills

Hour 2: Skill Set Reviews (all previous skills)
Listing and explanation of drills (selective drills for reinforcing skills)

Hour 3: Combination Drills
Listing and explanation of drills (selective drills for reinforcing skills)

Hour 4: Combination Drills
Listing and explanation of drills (selective drills for reinforcing skills)

Cool Down and Session Meeting

DAY FOUR
Pre-Instructional Warm-up and Stretching

Hour 1: Team Play (random drills)
Scoring and drill explanations

Hour 2: Team Play (random drills)
Scoring and drill explanations

Hour 3: Team play (competition)
Game play with realistic conditions (team verses team, scoring, refereeing, etc.)

Hour 4: Team Play (competition)
Game play with realistic conditions (team verse team, scoring, refereeing, etc.)

Continued on page 168

Figure 14.2. **Sports Camp Instructional Plan Format** *(continued from page 166)*

Cool Down and Session Meeting

Final Camp Meeting with Participants

Special Notes:

- If possible, the instruction/demonstration of skills (from Day One: Hour 1 to Day Three: Hour 3) should be done in front of the entire camp.

- Demonstrations should be by instructional staff members (not campers) that are proficient in that particular skill.

- The 45 minutes of drills and activities during the reinforcement period of each hour should be detailed out in an instructional plan provided to each clinician.

Time allotments for each drill as well as drill criteria should be presented in the instructional plan. All drills should be reviewed prior to the start of the overall summer sports camp by the head clinician and instructional staff.

- Break times should be strictly followed.

- Drills should be in ascending order of difficulty during reinforcement period of each hour with simple drills building to complex drills.

- During drills, instructional staff will provide positive corrective feedback.

Figure 14.2. **Sports Camp Instructional Plan Format** *(continued from page 167)*

MANAGING AND LEADING CAMP OPERATIONS

Overview

To begin the discussion of managing and leading a summer sports camp, the managerial idea of self-fulfilling prophecy becomes a relevant topic. The self-fulfilling prophecy is explained as

> the relationship between a leader's expectations and the resulting performance of subordinates. . . . Generally, it has been found that if a manager's expectations are high, productivity is likely to be high. On the other hand, if the manager's expectations are low, productivity is likely to be poor.[3]

With that said, it is essential that a camp administrator and/or the camp's head clinician establish behavioral policies that promote the safest possible camp environment, have strong commitment to the camp's mission and goals, convey professionalism, and follow all pre-established policies and operating procedures. While one might feel that these points could restrict one's enjoyment, the opposite is true. An atmosphere that stresses safety, professionalism, and commitment can also be fun within a cooperative, team feeling.

While discussed in Chapter 8's job description, it is important to restate that the most important instructional/leadership position during the summer sports camp is the head clinician. The head clinician could be categorized as the director of all camp activities and instruction. For the success of a head clinician, the following leadership points illustrate critical managerial concepts that should be adopted. The head clinician

- should always remember that he or she is in a position of leadership and control,

- encourages empowerment with accountability among the summer sports camp's instructors,

- does not act like he or she is above the law and policies and procedures do not apply to him or her,
- is willing to roll up his or her sleeves and assist camp instructors in any way possible while remembering not to sidestep a clinician's authority,
- is skilled at conflict resolution,
- supports innovation in instruction and camp tactics with his or her instructors,
- ensures ethical standards are being maintained,
- eliminates or minimizes environmental distractions to provide the best teaching and learning atmosphere,
- is adaptable and can think on the fly when it comes to adjusting instructional objectives,
- insists on inclusion for all participants despite skill level,
- shows a deep commitment to pre-established instructional goals,
- is a dynamic and charismatic ambassador for the summer sports camp,
- promotes teamwork in staff and participants, and
- is skilled in the use of formal authority.

Management and Leadership Tactics

There are other generic managerial and leadership elements that are universal to all summer instructional sports camps. They are as follows (in no specific order):

- High positive energy and encouragement: The environment set by the staff and clinicians involved in the camp is crucial to all the participants' learning and enjoyment. Camps can be a new-found experience for a young athlete and, by being new, could trigger some tension and fear. From the moment a participant arrives, the registration process, facilitation into groups, instruction, and post-camp activities must all be encouraging and friendly. Typically, the most anxiety for participants will come during the actual instruction and participation in activities and drills. Clinicians and instructors should at all times be as friendly, personable, and as supportive as possible while maintaining a professional manner to help athletes develop, correct, or enhance their talents.
- Provide activity breaks and rest periods: In cooperation with the summer sports camp's training and medical staff, appropriate breaks should be scheduled in all instructional sessions. These rest periods become of greater consequence in camps that are outdoors or in poorly air-conditioned facilities. There should be sufficient hydrating stations with water and prescribed sports drinks. Trainers (who should always be in attendance) can stop any camp session they see fit to allow for breaks. The camp training and medical staff are unconditionally in charge of the participants' health and safety. Their recommendations should be deemed absolute, without discussion.

Camp Tip

If a camp administrator is not the head clinician, there needs to be a strong relationship between the two parties. This symbiotic relationship is accomplished through open lines of communication.

- Have a structured, controlled camp atmosphere: Structure will convey professionalism as well as lessen campers' anxieties. Post schedules at sites whenever possible. Additionally, have precamp staff conferences to examine schedules, locations, activities, and job responsibilities. The more orderly the camp, the better flow and more constructive atmosphere the camp will have.

- Appreciate one's own leadership style: Because of the dynamic nature of the profession, camp administrators must willfully avoid a stagnant leadership style. The concept of one style and approach for all circumstances is outdated and will lead to poor group leadership. Camp administrators need to be situational evaluators of internal and external elements as well as people. In other words, camp leaders need to assess situations and choose an appropriate leadership response. That is the core foundation of situational leadership. Situational leaders are flexible in their observation of their surroundings. They look at every person, event, and environment as a distinct challenge requiring individual responses instead of planned reactions. In the simplest terms, for a camp administrator to become a situational leader, he or she needs to actively assess his or her surroundings and choose appropriate, decisive responses to maximize the camp's potential. The three basic leadership styles that are the foundation of situational leadership—autocratic/authoritarian, democratic/participative, and laissez faire/abdicative—are examined in Appendix 14.1.

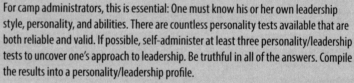

Camp Tip

For camp administrators, this is essential: One must know his or her own leadership style, personality, and abilities. There are countless personality tests available that are both reliable and valid. If possible, self-administer at least three personality/leadership tests to uncover one's approach to leadership. Be truthful in all of the answers. Compile the results into a personality/leadership profile.

- Utilize MBWA: MBWA is management by walking around. It is defined as "the technique that effective leaders use to stay informed about how well the strategy execution process is progressing."[4] By engaging camp staff and clinicians by walking around, a camp administrator can look for opportunities to (1) discuss camp goals, (2) assist in clinician development, (3) stress the importance of time management and keep on schedule, and (4) be on-hand to answer any and all questions. Even if a camp administrator is not acting as the head clinician, walk the facility and communicate with the participants. It will show loyalty and commitment to the camp's mission.

- Develop unity among staff and clinicians: While there are symbolic actions to develop unity among stakeholders, some real tactics could be as simple as providing each and every camp employee with camp t-shirts to wear at all camp activities. Additionally, have a group area for staff, administrators, and clinicians that has a daily hospitality table. This location can provide a needed break for all personnel as well as develop friendships and teamwork. Finally, as important as the beginning-of-the-day meeting is, consider having a wrapup session at the end of each camp day.

- Understand the importance of listening: To enhance the communication process and one's leadership abilities, stress the importance of strong listening skills (see Appendix 14.2).

- Fix-the-problem-first attitude: When issues arise, leaders need to act decisively to solve problems. Leaders do not shy away from problems. It is their function to resolve them. As the camp's leader, a camp administrator needs to look first for ways to resolve problems and then, if necessary, look for the true underlying reasons for the problem. Too many times, people in leadership roles focus on the reasons for an issue rather than focusing on solving it.

- Appreciate emotional intelligence: Emotional intelligence (which is detailed in Appendix 14.3) needs a leader's constant attention. Athletics involves emotions. As a camp administrator, one needs to recognize this fact and be prepared to exercise personal control as well as develop a strong sense of emotional empathy.

APPENDIX 14.1: Authoritarian/Autocratic, Democratic/Participative, Laissez Faire/Abdication

The most widely known of all leadership theories that can be reviewed by a camp administrator is based on the behavioral distinctions between authoritarian/autocratic, democratic/participative, and laissez faire/abdication. The following is a breakdown of these three universal styles.

Authoritarian/Autocratic

The authoritarian method of leadership is the inflexible employment of rightful power inherent in a position of management such as camp administrator or head clinician. The flow of decisions is from a top-down HR system in which all administrative decisions by a leader are absolute and unyielding. The style utilizes straightforward accountability expectations that are clear, logical, and comprehensible. The most common settings for the application of authoritarian leadership are military and medical settings that rely on orders given and carried out.

A distinct downfall of the authoritarian approach is as follows:

Leaders who are consistently authoritarian in style are not usually very popular, although they are prized in an emergency when quick, firm decisions are needed. . . . [I]n most situations group members do want their voices heard, especially when a decision directly affects them. This is not to say they want prolonged discussion that produces nothing more than "analysis paralysis" or that they don't think their leaders are capable. Rather, most group members just want their opinions heard and respected by their leaders.[5]

On the other hand, if a leader is respected and has a long track record of success and if the situation is receptive to this technique, the advantages range from timely completion of tasks to the focus of a single vision.

Once again, the principal drawback with the authoritarian/autocratic leadership approach is that personnel are made aware of what to do but not why they should be doing it. This leads to

- low personnel morale;
- workers following leader's orders to the letter, even if those commands are flawed; and
- possibly having staff and clinicians shun assignments, initiative, and originality.

Democratic/Participative

The democratic leadership approach to decision making is completely opposite from the authoritarian style.

> Structures that enable people at all levels to participate in decisions benefit from improved moral, reduced turnover, higher productivity, and better customer service. This is not to say that employees should have an opportunity to participate in decision making all the time. Such opportunities occur when the issue has a direct bearing on employees, there is time to get everyone's opinion, and the people participating are qualified in terms of knowledge and experience.[6]

This style accomplishes production and goal achievement through group agreement and acceptance. The most common use of the democratic style in our culture is through our governmental political system.

As with all leadership approaches, the environment in which a leader is operating will influence the style of leadership. Our society is founded and governed on the philosophical principles of democracy. From this perspective, one could assume that this doctrine is suitable for all facets of our lives. This assumption is unsound. For example, emergencies in our society would have disastrous consequences if the professional involved (say, a doctor, firefighter, or police officer) utilized the democratic leadership style. The best example of this for a camp would be in the case of a medical emergency. By the time the camp administrator finished polling everyone for their opinion, the situation might be considerably worse.

If the condition merits the employment of the democratic method, the benefits are unlimited. Some advantages include

- more contributions and information from a broader variety of individuals gives a decision maker a different perspective,
- a sense of group confidence and morale,

- operational personnel having an invested interest in the choices and consequences of camp decisions, and
- a re-energized camp emphasis on objectives.

Laissez Faire/Abdicated

The final leadership style of laissez faire/abdicated is best described as a profile of leadership that is "the avoidance of leadership altogether. Important actions are delayed, responsibility is ignored, and power and influence go unutilized. One common measure of leadership reflects laissez-faire styles with this statement: 'The leader avoids getting involved when important issues arise.'[7] From a camp perspective, this leadership attitude is very irrational, disjointed, and should rarely be used. This technique has camp personnel setting goals and individualizing work ethics. With no direction, camp personnel will set their own agendas, in their own timeframes, and by their own guidelines. The only possible circumstance in which this approach could be utilized would be in a leisurely environment where achieving goals within a given timeframe is not a priority. The major disadvantages of this approach are as follows:

- It is careless and makes little effort to guide and organize a group
- Typically inadequate in camp conditions because the group lacks focus and confronts problems in a chaotic manner
- Leaves personnel to establish objectives, individualize camp ethics, and functioning policies
- Provides literally no direction to camp personnel; clinicians, staff members, and participants will decide their own itineraries, in their own timeframes, and by their own parameters.

APPENDIX 14.2: LEADERSHIP COMMUNICATION—LISTENING

Being an effective communicator is essential to being a competent leader. Being able to impart critical information and to guide people is typically the initial characteristic that people associate with leadership communication. The other side, which is perhaps the most overlooked and neglected skill of leadership, is listening. For a camp's success, active listening to camp personnel is often a more critical function of leadership than being a great speaker. Listening in a sports camp can refresh personal relationships, gather information for decision making, and function as a condition for productivity and rewards.

Ineffectual Listening Habits

There can be many causes of ineffectual listening. Regardless of whether the barriers to listening are environmental, physiological, or psychological, the identification and intentional elimination of these listening blocks is critical. Factors of faulty listening can encompass the following:

- Fact-listening: Analyzing messages only for facts, not intended meanings.
- Thinking of an argument: Instead of listening and concentrating on the message, a poor listener diverts his or her attention to rebuttals and counter attacks.
- Being critical of semantics: Being narrowly focused on semantic (meaning of words) misinterpretations and misuses and concentrating on the technical instrument of communication rather than the themes and ideas being communicated.
- Scrutinizing delivery: Focusing attention on the method of delivery (the how) rather than the substance and content of information transmitted (the what).
- Frozen evaluation: Having a negative preconceived concept of a message and/or speaker will repress information being communicated.
- Pretending to listen: Faking alertness.
- Taking detailed notes: Writing notes obsessively is detrimental to comprehension because meanings and nuances are lost.
- Rushing communication: Impatient and often self-centered rushing of the speaker displays a bored, ineffective communication environment.
- Hearing, not listening: Hearing and listening are overlapping but different concepts. Hearing is the physical action of sounds, while listening is the reception, understanding, assimilation, and retention of information.
- Daydreaming: Self-explanatory.

Camp Tip

To become mindful of ineffectual listening habits, consciously observe as many conversations as possible and look for clues of communication breakdowns. From those witnessed communication failures, one can become aware of one's own conversations and ineffectual habits.

Effective Listening Habits

The 2002 article "Cheers, Ears—How to Listen Well" illustrates some insightful techniques that will help a summer sports camp administrator become an effective listener. Good listening tactics that can be adopted include the following:

Receiver On: Proper listening is active rather than passive. You need to actively decide to give someone a damn good listening to. You can't do this without setting aside quality time for it. The person you are listening to must know that, for the duration of your conversation, they are your priority. There is nothing more flattering than giving your undivided attention.

Transmitter Off: Strange as it may seem, some people think that it's perfectly possible to listen while carrying on talking continuously. . . . [Y]ou need to put all your thoughts, concerns, and feelings temporarily to one side and concentrate completely on understanding the thoughts, concerns, and feelings of the other person.

Tune In: When someone talks they will have a host of assumptions—many of which you may not share. You therefore need to use who, what, why, where, when, and how to continually check the meaning of what they're saying.

Volume Up: People will talk about anything given the chance. It's perfectly okay to ask them to talk about what's most on your mind.

Echoing: This is a subtle way of getting someone to tell you more about what you want to hear. Whatever word, phrase or even sentence you repeat, the talker will automatically tell you more about it.

Check Feelings: Ask someone what they think and they'll tell you one thing; ask them what they feel and they'll usually tell you something completely different. If you're looking for the truth, asking for feelings will get you there a lot quicker.

Playback: At the end of the conversation, summarize what the person has just said. If you get it wrong, they'll correct you; if you get it right, they'll feel they've been given a good hearing.[8]

> ## Camp Tip
> Listening takes practice and effort. An exercise technique that highlights listening is to see how many times in a conversation with a subordinate one can say "so what you are saying is. . ." By practicing this method of verbatim message repetition, an individual can strengthen his or her listening effectiveness. This listening tactic also reassures the subordinate that they are being listened to and their message is important.

Nonverbal Listening

Another aspect of listening does not require verbal understanding. For a camp administrator to become an even more effective listener-leader, he or she needs to be an interpreter of nonverbal communication. How can a camp administrator become a skillful observer of nonverbal communication? First and most significantly, an effective leader realizes that nonverbal behaviors are situational, personalized, and not necessarily on the surface. Strong nonverbal interpreters know that

> people sometimes say one thing and mean something else. So watch as you listen to be sure that the speaker's eyes, body, and face are sending the same message as the verbal message. If something seems out of sync, get it cleared up by asking questions.[9]

Second, strong communicators suppress their own opinions and feelings while evaluating and interpreting nonverbal body language. Finally, all strong listeners dissect and notice facial expressions and eye movement. There are thousands of illustrative expressions; the possibility for misinterpretation is great. For a leader to become capable of analyzing facial expressions, he or she must realize that it is a personal discipline that must have constant practice.

The following list of five items provides a foundation for reading and distinguishing nonverbal behavior.

1. Personal appearance: People's clothing and grooming present insight into their attitude and their message. As with all nonverbal cues, personal appearances are situational and should be evaluated by their appropriateness in a particular setting.

2. Personal space: An important signal of nonverbal communication is the maintenance of space between speaker and listener. For instance, the distance can indicate comfort and confidence or uneasiness and doubt (e.g., an intimate distance of 1-2 feet, a personal distance of 2-5 feet, a social distance of 5-10 feet, or a public distance of 10 or more feet).

3. Posture: Posture is another powerful nonverbal message. For example, if a speaker's posture is brittle and restrictive, it could be determined that the speaker is uncomfortable. Conversely, if a subordinate's physique is slumped and totally relaxed, boredom or apathy could be conveyed.

4. Appendages: The movement (or lack of movement) in body components such as arms, hands, feet, and legs can be important signals. For example, a stationary person with arms folded across the chest could be conveying defensiveness.

5. Timing: The timing of a person's entrance into a setting can disclose important nonverbal messages. If one is inexcusably tardy, a message of indifference and animosity could be conveyed, while punctuality could communicate interest and courtesy.

The list of nonverbal cues is endless. The assessment of those elements should be based on the circumstances and the individuals involved. Changing a camp administrator into a person who can benefit from careful attention to both verbal and nonverbal cues is often difficult. It takes a careful and calculated concentration. However, the payoff for this focused effort is vast. This active technique fosters personnel retention, as well as enables a camp administrator to digest all information confidently, which is essential to effective leadership.

Camp Tip

Communication is a two-way process. A camp administrator should continually observe his or her own nonverbal messages. Throughout the day, periodically stop and dissect nonverbal behavior, examining personal appearance, personal spacing, posture, and timing. From the observations, determine if the nonverbal behaviors are appropriate for the situation and communication that is being attempted.

APPENDIX 14.3: LEADERSHIP AND EMOTIONAL INTELLIGENCE

A widely studied topic in the field of managerial leadership is the concept of emotional intelligence. "Emotional intelligence refers to verbal and non-verbal abilities to recognize one's own emotions and those of others, understanding them, and employ them in dealing with the demands and pressures of interpersonal communication."[10] The two features of emotional intelligence that need clarifying are (1) a leader's internal assessment and command of his or her emotional state (self-awareness) and (2) the capacity to determine the emotional state of subordinates. Both of these elements require practice but can have a major impact on a camp administrator's success.

The subsequent points are foundational components in developing both internal emotional awareness and external emotional sensitivity in others.

- An emotionally intelligent leader is in tune with the camp's culture and the influence that culture can have on one's own emotional condition as well as the personnel's emotional state. If a camp's culture favors an agitated or highly charged emotional environment, a camp administrator must construct initiatives to offset this type of atmosphere. Conversely, if a camp's culture is dispirited or apathetic, a camp administrator will need to cultivate objectives to offset this culture emotional impact.

- An emotionally intelligent leader appreciates the fact that every individual (including themselves) can be, and often is, affected by concerns outside one's normal work environment. External variables that can have an effect on one's emotional state can include financial concerns, family obligations, illness, educational advancement efforts, or a combination of all of these. Knowing that the factors exist and understanding their impact on one's emotional state is a key characteristic of being an effective leader.

- To get an accurate picture of a person's emotional state, a camp administrator should develop a level of comfort with the coaches, administrators, and staff while maintaining professionalism and leadership authority. These types of associations, while often time consuming to develop, can yield countless camp benefits, including a heightened awareness of the camp members' emotional makeup and tolerance.

- An emotionally intelligent leader realizes that emotions can be contagious in an organization. The power of emotions is even more noticeable if they are generated by the leader. Understanding this, a camp administrator should attempt to avoid large emotional swings that could have a harmful effect on the camp's personnel.

- A skilled, emotionally intelligent leader always knows to avoid making camp decisions (no matter how minor or impactful) while under the influence of strong emotions. The classic example of this is when a camp administrator is angry about a subordinate's behavior or actions. In these cases, an emotionally intelligent leader will step back from the situation, get control of frustration and anger, and then assess which course of action to take. Simply stated, leaders need to maintain emotional composure and stability when making camp decisions.

Special Note: While cultivating an empathetic ability to determine a person's emotional state is a critical component of summer sports camp leadership, it is not a substitute for bypassing experts in assisting or even solving emotional issues. If a camp administrator encounters a subordinate who is having emotional issues and elevated levels of stress, one duty is to get that individual to a professional specialist immediately. In these cases it is also advisable to inform all supervisors in the chain of command about the situation.

ENDNOTES

1. Katz, J., & Green, R. (2014). *Entrepreneurial small business* (4th edition), p. 538. New York, NY: McGraw-Hill Irwin.

2. Cruickshank, D., Jenkins, D., & Metcalf, K. (2003). *The art of teaching* (3rd edition), pp. 139-140. New York, NY: McGraw-Hill.

3. Rue, L. W., & Byars, L. L. (2009). *Management: Skills and application* (13th edition), p. 287. New York, NY: McGraw-Hill/Irwin.

4. Thompson, A. A., Peteraf, M. A., Strickland, A. J., & Gamble, J. E. (2014). *Crafting and executing strategy: The quest for competitive advantage: Concepts and cases* (19th edition), p. 359. New York, NY: McGraw-Hill/Irwin.

5. Renzetti, C. M., & Curran, D. J. (1998). *Living sociology,* p. 144. Needham Heights, MA: Allyn and Bacon.

6. Charney, C. (2006). *The leader's tool kit: Hundreds of tips and techniques for developing the skill you need,* p. 30. New York, NY: AMACOM.

7. Colquitt, J. A., LePine, J. A., & Wesson, M. J. (2009). *Organizational behavior: Improving performance and commitment in the workplace,* p. 488. New York, NY: McGraw-Hill/Irwin.

8. Browning, G. (2002) Cheers, ears – How to listen well. *People Management, 8*(24), 106.

9. Lussier, R. N., & Achua, C. F. (2007). *Leadership: Theory, application, and skill development* (3rd edition), p. 204. Mason, OH: Thompson South-Western.

10. Chelladuria, P. (2006). *Human resource management in sport and recreation* (2nd edition), p. 56. Champaign, IL: Human Kinetics.

15

Instruction

INSTRUCTION IN SUMMER SPORTS CAMPS

Overview

Before instruction methods can be presented, it is necessary to look at a general list of coaching/teaching viewpoints for sports camps. This listing is common to all sports camps, can be applicable or philosophical, and is in no particular order.

1. A camp's instructional principles should highlight athlete development rather than merely a series of skill drills and exercises. Development is more in line with long-term improvement and retention while drill sequencing is more associated with short-term behaviors and actions.

2. Every training activity should concentrate on instructional goals. Doing a drill for drill's sake rather than purposed instruction is a misuse of precious camp time.

3. If the camp is in a multifunctional facility, with excellent clinicians and a sizeable volume of campers, consider a group rotation approach (or stations) to stress specific skill development. This type of instruction also depends on the particular sport.

4. When teaching precise skills, the use of teaching cues in established acronyms (either original for the particular camp or universally

recognized sport acronyms) can be a valuable tool to help campers retain information.

5. When developing a group's overall instructional plan, it is important that athlete development be through a step-by-step system. The structure should take the camper from base level skills to higher complex abilities through a series of well- constructed, gradual increasing drills, exercises, or applications. Powerful camp instruction has a coherent flow and pacing within each learning session. "There should be an overall logic to the manner in which a lesson proceeds, and that logic should be discernible to students."[1]

6. When forming instruction plans, utilize the camp's most valuable asset: its people. The camp's clinicians can contribute new instructional

ideas, new technologies, working knowledge of the sport, tactical intelligence, etc.

7. Never undervalue the importance of contingency plans and ideas. Rarely in life does everything work out precisely as designed. For a superior camp, be prepared for potential and unexpected events with reliable contingency plans.

8. The camp should always be designed for equal participation by all participants, regardless of their skill level. All training sessions should be arranged accordingly. In the plainest language, the camp should have a student-centered philosophy that emphasizes fairness.

9. Never underestimate the significance of "fuzzies" (also known as "at-a-boys"/"at-a-girls"). These minor comments by a clinician can have an influential, if not overwhelming impact, on young developing athletes who admire a seasoned clinician.

10. At a session's beginning, state all teaching and instructional policies and procedures. Discuss the camp's expectations and guidelines continually throughout the session. Always remember that the clinician in charge controls the instructional environment for a group. It is his or her obligation to maintain the strongest conceivable professionalism and management in the group's environment. Be familiar with all campers and their conduct. If issues arise, adhere to pre-established procedures and keep all supervisors well-informed of potential problems.

11. Remember that enthusiasm generates enthusiasm. A clinician's attitude and energy will percolate throughout the group.

© Piksel | Dreamstime.com

Special Note: A financial and instructional challenge can emerge when discussing the balancing of participant numbers with personalized teaching goals. From a financial perspective, the camp will want to take advantage of capacity limits for maximum monetary returns. From an instructional standpoint, clinicians and instructors will want somewhat smaller sessions to emphasize individualized attention. If open communication and cooperative planning are utilized, both objectives can be accomplished in the camp's operations. Camp administrators need to value quality instructional limitations, while instructors and clinicians need to recognize the importance of reaching financial objectives.

Camp Tip

A core feature of the camp that should be stressed to all participants, instructional staff, and administrators is the development of a sense of citizenship and community in the camp environment. While competition might occur in drills and game situations, sportsmanship should always be highlighted. Noncompliance with these obligations should immediately be addressed and corrective action taken.

Precamp Instructional Assessment

Prior to placing athletes into camp groups, the instructional staff will need to determine the level of participants' skills and competitive abilities. Consider using a pre-instruction questionnaire, which can be distributed during the registration process or during initial camp activities. Quantitative factors, such as age, grade, number of years involved in the sport, and a breakdown of progression levels, could be elements used to verify a participant's placement into summer sports camp groups. Questions based on specific skills (on a numerical scale 1–5) could be asked to allow participants to elaborate on areas of strengths and weaknesses. Once groupings are determined, in-camp assessments through firsthand observations by instructional staff should be used to move participants up or down to the suitable skill grouping. To avoid possible embarrassment, any camp athlete being moved down into a lower skill group needs to be tactfully informed and moved as promptly and as quietly as possible. Recommendations on moving an athlete up into an advanced skill group should take into account emotional maturity as well as skill level.

Depending on the camp's sport, a pre-instruction fitness evaluation of all participants could be a necessity. The physical fitness evaluation, which should be administered by the camp's athletic trainers and medical staff, should be directed at aerobic, strength, and flexibility elements that are fundamental in that specific sport. Instrumentation and documentation should be used. All results should be discussed with participants and made a permanent component of each camper's file.

Teaching Techniques in Sport

While each sport will have its own set of instructional techniques that are unique and distinctive, there are general teaching tactics that are universal to all instruction.

The following section highlights the most prominent teaching strategies that can be adapted to summer sports camp instruction.

Rapport Development

To enrich camp participants' learning and overall experience, a clinician needs to develop a rapport with his or her instructional group and individual campers.

> Rapport creates trust, allowing you to build a *psychological bridge* to someone. The conversation is likely to be more positive and comfortable when two people are "in sync" with each other. Just as we tend to like someone who shares our interests, we are also unconsciously driven to like a person when she "appears as we do."[2]

This psychological bridge is critical in communicating important sports knowledge. Simply stated, a clinician with a likable rapport that creates trust produces an environment for teaching and learning. Additionally, clinicians should take advantage of down-time opportunities to develop their connection with the camp group. Remember, every minute of camp time is valuable, break times included.

Participant Engagement

To engage summer sports camp participants, a clinician can adopt or modify the following points:

- Involve all students in the act, not just any one student or group. Avoid concentrating on only those who appear most interested or responsive, sometimes referred to as the "chosen few."

- Keep students alert by calling on them randomly, asking questions, and calling on an answerer, circulating from group to group during team learning activities and frequently checking on the progress on individual students.

- Maintain constant visual surveillance of the entire class, even when talking to or working with individual or small group of students and when meeting a classroom visitor at the door.

- Move around the room. Be on top of potential misbehavior and quietly redirect student attention before the misbehavior occurs or gets out of control.

© Luckybusiness | Dreamstime.com

- During direct instruction try to establish eye contact with each student about once every minute. It initially may sound impossible to do, but it is not; this skill can be developed with practice.[3]

Block, Random, and Combination Training

Block training techniques (also called *closed skills training*)

are performed in stable or predictable environments; because of this, more consistent form is desired, even for outcome specific skills. For closed skills, instructional strategies should assist students in fixating on a specific form that is successful for each student.[4]

Random training (*tactical awareness training*) should enhance block training in a developing athlete.

Tactical awareness, critical for game performance, is the ability to identify tactical problems that arise during a game and to respond appropriately. . . The link between skills and tactics enables students to learn about a game and improve their performance, especially because game tactics provide the opportunity for applying same-related motor skills.[5]

As discussed, with block training, skills are broken down and reinforced with continuous repetition of each skill by the athlete. While repetition training is considered the building block of skills necessary to compete, the drills do not reinforce competition situations. An athlete who is solely block trained will have absolutely no success in a competitive situation due to the fact that he or she will not know the entirety of the sport, just its parts. Conversely, only providing campers with random training without developing the foundational skills would be totally impractical. The instructional connectors between block or repetition training and random or competitive training are called *combination drills*.

Combination drills take multiple skills that have been developed through block training and place them in game-like sequences. These game-like sequences are components of the competition, not the entire competitive sport. In a perfect instructional plan, every combination drill will connect foundational skills with competitive situations. For developmental campers, which is one of the target markets for a summer sports camp, it is a way to have them mentally construct and connect the whole from the parts.

Once again, while scheduling is important for a camp's instruction, training components and drills should be considered flexible inside each session due to different skill sets and abilities. Each divisional clinician should have the ability to add or delete time from a drill or to enlarge drills with different instructional variations—with the head clinician's knowledge and approval, of course.

Direct Instructional Approach

A camp can apply a direct instructional approach to lead participants through skills development.

Camp Tip

The idea of fun should be included into as many summer sports camp functions as possible while still achieving instructional goals. The assortment and design of participant activities, especially block training drills, should be done with both objectives in mind. This philosophy of fun is relevant for all participants at all levels (novice to elite).

The direct instructional strategy lays out a simple, four-phase process for maximizing skill acquisition.

1. *Modeling:* The skill is modeled by the teacher, who thinks aloud while performing the skill.

2. *Direct practice:* The teacher uses questions to lead students through the steps and to help them see the reasons behind the steps.

3. *Guided practice:* Students generate their own leading questions while working through the steps; the teacher observes, coaches, and provides feedback.

4. *Independent practice:* Finally, students work through more examples on their own.[6]

Cooperative and Competitive Learning

For camps, a fundamental concept of instruction relates to the balance of cooperative learning and competitive learning. In their text *Foundations of Education*, Allan Ornstein and Daniel Levine describe cooperative and competitive learning as follows:

> The idea of **cooperative learning** is to change the traditional structure by reducing competition and increasing cooperation among students, thus diminishing possible hostility and tension among students and raising academic achievement. This does not mean that competition has no place in the classroom or school. The chief advocates of cooperation tell us that competition can be used successfully to improve performance on simple drill activities and speed-related tasks . . . in low anxiety games and on the athletic field. Under the right conditions, competition can be a source of fun, excitement, and motivation. In cooperative learning, however, competition takes second place. According to a review of research, cooperation among participants helps build (1) positive and coherent personal identity, (2) self-actualization and mental health, (3) knowledge and trust of one another, (4) communication with one another, (5) acceptance and support of one another, and (6) wholesome relationships with a reduced amount of conflict. The data also suggest that cooperation and group learning are considerably more effective in fostering these social and interpersonal skills than are competitive or individualistic efforts.[7]

The balance between cooperative learning and competitive learning environments is totally up to the camp administrator and/or head clinician. Factors such as age, skill level, camp philosophy, goals, and sport will be relevant in making the determination of balance between the two instructional approaches. Remember, cooperative and competitive learning are not mutually exclusive. They should be blended in a way to maximize the learning experience for the campers.

Camp Tip

The intensity of competition in camp instruction relates to the internal motivation of the camp athletes themselves as well as the external motivation provided by the clinicians. If the external rewards provided by the clinicians are highly prized, the intensity will increase greatly.

Demonstrations

Demonstrations are a key element in any camp operation and instructional method. Whether the clinician is demonstrating the skill or supervising another clinician demonstrator, there are some basic components that must be emphasized. In the textbook *Physical Education Methods for Classroom Teachers*, some basic demonstration concepts are explained.

When you demonstrate a skill, you focus the children's attention on the lesson's objectives. Then after they can visualize this focus, the verbal instruction you give will take on enhanced meaning. When breaking down a task into components, demonstrate it in sequence and demonstrate it more than once. To demonstrate effectively,

1. make sure everyone can see you by checking that no one is blocked by another child, too far away, or blinded by sunlight;

2. show the whole action first, then feature the one part you're focusing on for the lesson, and, finally, show the whole action again;

3. show the skill at normal speed, then in slow motion; and

4. be sure to tell the students what they should focus on while watching (the cue word or phrase).[8]

Team Camp Instruction

If considering a team camp concept in a sports camp, there are specific decisions (administrative and instructional) that need to be determined.

1. Will the team camp be a combination of team instruction and tournament play or will the camp be structured as a competitive tournament only? If a combination is employed, what percentage of camp time will be selected for instruction and what percentage of camp time will be for competition?

2. Will teams be constructed randomly from a general pool of campers or will teams be constructed prior to camp (junior/senior high, junior Olympic, etc.)? If the teams are assembled from a broad-spectrum pool of participants, what will be the factors for grouping athletes into teams?

3. For the competitive component of a team sports camp, what will be the layout of tournament play? Will the competition be single elimination, double elimination, multilevel, round-robin, or head to head? Who and which factors will govern the seeding and team placements? Does the competitive outline agree with the facility and time constraints of the camp?

4. Who will coach each team? Since most athletic associations, whether educational or national (AAU, JOs, etc.), have specified regulations about off-season contact by regular team coaches, what will be the instructional staff needs? What will be the coaching structure of each team—head coach, assistants, and managers?

Camp Tip

For whatever reason, if a camp clinician feels he or she lacks the ability to demonstrate a skill, finding a surrogate demonstrator is important. However, the controlling clinician should conduct the instruction by regulating the demonstrator with verbal cues and instructional feedback.

5. If instruction is an ingredient of the camp, how will it be delivered? Will it be by the head clinician's assessments of each team's capabilities and then tailoring instruction based on that evaluation? Will it be a generic instructional plan that is used by all teams in the camp?

> **Camp Tip**
>
> After instructional and competitive sessions are over and campers have finished drills and activities, a fun and educational pastime is to have a closing competition using willing clinicians as participants. Depending on the sport, the purpose of such an in-camp event is to reinforce all of the skills learned by participants through observing competition or high-level play. As with participants, all safety factors should be followed for instructors (camp insurances, warm-up, equipment, etc.). Under no circumstances should a clinician be forced to take part in such activities.

ENDNOTES

1. Marzano, R. (2007). *The art and science of teaching: A comprehensive framework for effective instruction,* p. 112. Alexandria, VA: Association for Supervision and Curriculum Development.
2. Lieberman, D. (2000). *Get anyone to do anything and never feel powerless again: Psychological secrets to predict, control, and influence every situation,* p. 7. New York, NY: St. Martin's Press.
3. Callahan, J., Clark, L., & Kellough, R. (2002). *Teaching in the middle and secondary schools* (7th edition), p. 166. Upper Saddle River, NJ: Prentice Hall Merrill.
4. Griffey, D. C., & Houser, L. D. (2007). *Designing effective instructional tasks for physical education and sports,* p. 3. Champaign, IL: Human Kinetics.
5. Mitchell, S. A., Oslin, J. L., & Griffin, L. L. (2006). *Teaching sport concepts and skills* (2nd edition), p. 8. Champaign, IL: Human Kinetics.
6. Silver, H. Strong, R., & Perini, M. (2007). *The strategic teacher: Selecting the right research-based strategy for every lesson,* p. 35. Upper Saddle River, NJ: Pearson.
7. Ornstein, A., & Levine, D. (2003). *Foundations of education* (8th edition), p. 442. Boston, MA: Houghton Mifflin.
8. Pettifor, B. (1999). *Physical education methods for classroom teachers,* p. 62. Champaign, IL: Human Kinetics.

CHAPTER

16

Post Administration

© Michaeljung | Dreamstime.com

INTRODUCTION

It cannot be stated too strongly: A camp is not over just because the campers have departed. The consequence of closing down an operation correctly should be a significant priority for all camps. To not complete this aspect of the camp would be comparable to tripping at the end of a race. Matters such as surveying, financial reporting, and branding are all central elements to follow through with to formally close the operation.

CAMPER SURVEYS

At the conclusion of each camp, surveying the campers informally through walk-around discussions and formally through an end-of-camp written survey is a sound continuous improvement function. Ask campers about their experiences at camp and what other services and training they may perhaps want in the future. If the parents are involved, solicit their assessments.

General Survey Rules and Procedures

A survey is "a method of collecting primary data in which information is gathered by communicating with a representative sample of people."[1] In effect, surveys are tools the camp administrator can utilize to collect crucial information about the operation.

This information will be the foundation of future camp decisions. While the workings of scientific research and survey instrumentation are complex, some straightforward survey guidelines can help ensure the data given will be as accurate, timely, and valuable as possible.

The first underlying issue in discussing survey research relates to *response rate.* Response rate is the percentage of individuals approached who completed a survey. The greater the response rate, the more accurate the data collected. For example, imagine a camp has a total of 500 campers and 300 completed the end-of-camp survey. The survey response rate was 60%—or conversely, a *40% non-respondent error.* In normal research projects, a 60% response rate would be considered exceptionally strong. However, with the camp environment being a captive audience, a near 100% response rate can be achieved. To accomplish this, the camp should include in its structure the final activity of completing the survey while the campers and parents are still at the camp's location. Once campers and parents leave the facility, the response rate will decrease drastically.

Another core recommendation to enhance the value of survey information is to select specific camp topics to ask respondents in the survey. A camp administrator, along with staff, clinicians, and administrators, should gather data on vital operational areas that are essential components of the camp. The selection of different categories must be balanced with the size limits of the survey instrument and the populations being surveyed. Simply put, one should try to get the maximum information without making the survey so cumbersome that respondents just complete it to leave the camp. As a general rule, if the survey consistently needs more than five minutes to complete, it may be too long.

While an undemanding numerical rating scale (1-5 with related descriptions) is simple and easy to understand, each survey should furnish an opportunity for respondents to narratively explain a particular summer sports camp item that may or may not be categorized in the survey. Additionally, to minimize data-handling and counting errors, multiple personnel should be involved in the tabulation of data. With this said, a basic checks-and-balances counting system should be developed.

In Figure 16.1 a camp survey template is given.

PRECISION OF FINANCIAL REPORTING

When closing down a camp, financial statements should be constructed that accurately represent the entire camp operation. These financial statements should be circulated to all relevant personnel.

The camp's system will determine the simplicity or complexity of constructing financial statements (income statements, balance sheets, statement of cash flow, etc.). Most computer software systems (like Quickbooks) can tabulate end-of-month reports at a moment's notice. Year-end tax forms and IRS reporting could be somewhat more difficult. For this reason, a summer sports camp administrator may consider outsourcing this function to an independent CPA. Additionally, if the summer camp is an

A 1 to 5 scale:

1 = Poor

2 = Below Average

3 = Average

4 = Above Average

5 = Excellent

Rate the following aspects of XYZ's Summer Sports Camp and your experience. Circle one answer only.

1. How would you rate the registration process?

Poor	Below Avg.	Avg.	Above Avg.	Excellent
1	2	3	4	5

What could be done to improve XYZ's Summer Camp registration process?

_____

_____

_____

_____

2. How would you rate the camp facilities?

Poor	Below Avg.	Avg.	Above Avg.	Excellent
1	2	3	4	5

What facility features would you like to see for next year's summer camp?

_____

_____

_____

_____

3. Rate the following camp instruction elements:

Element	Poor	Below Avg.	Avg.	Above Avg.	Excellent
New learning from instruction	1	2	3	4	5
Quality of drills	1	2	3	4	5
Quality of competition	1	2	3	4	5
Instructor's knowledge	1	2	3	4	5
Instructor's helpfulness	1	2	3	4	5
Individual attention	1	2	3	4	5
Demonstrations	1	2	3	4	5

From the above instructional elements, what suggestions would you make?

_____

_____

_____

Continued on next page.

Figure 16.1. **Summer Sports Camp Survey Template**

How would you rate XYZ's medical/training staff?

Poor	Below Avg.	Avg.	Above Avg.	Excellent
1	2	3	4	5

What treatments did you receive?

_____

_____

_____

4. What is your overall opinion of XYZ's Summer Sports Camp?

Poor	Below Avg.	Avg.	Above Avg.	Excellent
1	2	3	4	5

How did you hear about XYZ's camp? Circle all that apply

TV   Radio   Newspaper   Flyers   Brochure   Signs/Posters

Coach's Recommendation   Other Players   Other _____

What camp session(s) did you attend?

_____

_____

_____

Other comments:

_____

_____

_____

* If the summer sports camp is an overnight camp, questions relating to auxiliary activities, quality of accommodations, and food program should be added.

Figure 16.1. **Summer Sports Camp Survey Template** *(Continued from page 189)*

element of an institution (e.g., high school, college, etc.), reporting responsibilities dictated by those organizations and their governing bodies need to be followed.

Bank Accounts

A camp administrator should close or suspend its camp bank account immediately after all camp distributions and receipts have been accounted for. For the reliability and financial safety of all who are involved with the camp, it is important to empty the account, halt all transactions, and document bank account closure.

Inventory Control

An area that can have a great impact on a camp's profit margin is the operation's inventory. To manage this element of camp, the following clear-cut formula should be employed for each and every type of equipment and camp-specific assets.

Beginning Inventory + Camp Purchases − Ending Inventory = Inventory Used

The best situation is when a camp's beginning inventory plus its in-camp purchases equals its ending inventory. For long-term capital expenditures that are typically high dollar value, this is crucial, but regrettably is not always the case. It is critical that a thorough camp inventory be taken prior to the camp's operation (which could be the ending inventory from a previous camp) as well as an exhaustive ending inventory. Any discrepancies, which can range from equipment or supplies damaged through regular use, missing equipment, distributed items, and loaned items, need to be investigated and account for.

PERMANENT FILING SYSTEM

The archiving of e-files and hardcopy files should be a post-camp priority. For easy access, these files should be securely stored and separated from other athletic organization files. See Chapter 7's "General Concepts for Filing Systems" for filing details and archiving.

BRAND DEVELOPMENT

Just because the summer sports camp is over does not mean that there are no opportunities to promote the camp's brand awareness. Frequently communicate with camp alumni and their families throughout the year. These informative communications can enlarge positive word-of-mouth advertising and provide a summer sports camp with a competitive advantage through a devoted clientele base.

Social Media

The power of social media is almost unimaginable. For summer sports camps, it should be a foundational concept when it comes to retaining current customers, building the camp's brand awareness, and networking to develop new clients. Every single camper who attends any session offered by the organization should be automatically included in the camp's Facebook/Twitter network. This type of focused database of Facebook friends or Twitter tweets can have a large influence on the number of people who know about the camp. With the permission of the people in the photos, camp pictures

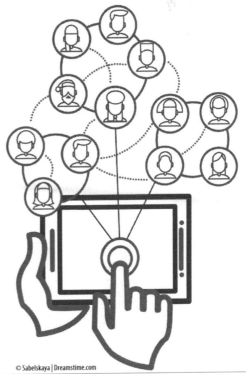

© Sabelskaya | Dreamstime.com

could be posted, clinician profiles displayed, brochures published, etc. The possible uses for social media are unbounded.

Twitter and Facebook have proven to be useful channels for connecting with both customers and media, but there are many others. LinkedIn was launched in May 2003 as a "grown-up" version of Facebook, appealing to a more business-minded audience by focusing on professional rather than personal relationships.[2]

From this statement, it is important to employ social media for not only the camp's direct customer based, but also any possible strategic partners, consultants, and specialists.

INTERNAL FEEDBACK

Solicit feedback from camp administrators, staff, and clinicians; if financially feasible, have a final camp gathering that combines social interaction with information gathering. Within the goal of collecting feedback, ask direct questions related to the improvement of camp operations, the increasing value given to campers, and the enlargement of the operation.

Camp Celebration

As mentioned above, an enjoyable way to end a camp is to have a special gathering that shows all personnel their value to the camp. These get-togethers could be as modest as a pizza party in the summer sports camp's facility to a full-fledged formal dinner. Whatever method selected, it is always important to show your people that they are appreciated and respected.

ENDNOTES

1. Zigmund, W. (2003). *Essentials of marketing research* (2nd edition), p. 141. Mason, OH: Thomson South-Western.
2. Argenti, P. (2013). *Corporate communication* (6th edition), *p. 162*. New York, NY: McGraw-Hill Irwin.

Index

About the Author

Richard Leonard, PhD, is an associate professor of business administration at Flagler College in Tallahassee, Florida. His primary teaching focus is in strategic management with secondary instruction in human resource management and marketing. In addition to his duties at Flagler College, Leonard is an adjunct professor of sport management at the United States Sports Academy (USSA). His principal areas of instruction at USSA are in doctoral and graduate level courses in strategic management, human resource management, event planning, fundraising, and marketing.

Leonard's main academic concentration over the past 10 years has been publishing textbooks. Leonard's textbook titles, all from FiT Publishing, include *The Administrative Side of Coaching: Applying Business Concepts to Athletic Program Administration and Coaching* (1st ed. 2005, 2nd ed., 2008), *Fundraising for Sport and Athletics* (2012), and *Principle of Sport Administration* (2013). Additionally, he has written numerous sport administration articles. These articles (published by the American Volleyball Coaches Association, the governing body of the sport) encompass every aspect of sport management, including planning, organization, human resource management, and strategic management.

Leonard's experience in summer camps (both recreational and athletic) is extensive. At the Jewish Community Center (JCC) of Pinellas County in St. Petersburg, Florida, he was a summer camp divisional counselor (1986), community center activities director (1986-1987), and community center program coordinator (1988-1991). The summer recreational camps, which were the centerpiece of the JCC's operation, had door-to-door transportation, a wide variety of on-campus activities, and daily/weekly off-campus trips and events throughout Florida and the southeastern US. The JCC summer camps were considered one of the finest recreational camps in central Florida. As an NCAA Division I volleyball coach, Leonard's sports camps over a five-year period grew an amazing 400%. As the owner/operator and head clinician, the summer sports camps had traditional day camps, specialty skill sessions, coaches' clinics, and team camps. These elite camps operated at a 10-1 ratio and provided high-level instruction to different ages and skill levels. Additionally, during his coaching career, Leonard worked as a clinician at numerous high school and college camps and coaches clinics.

Leonard has a bachelor's degree in accounting from Robert Morris University, an MBA in management from Florida Metropolitan University—Tampa College, and a PhD in administration and management from Walden University. He has certifications in strategic management and leadership from the American Management Association as well as certifications in professional learning, collaborative learning, and classroom management.